THE BILL OF RIGHTS
FOR PEOPLE IN PAIN

1. I have the *right* to live a full and happy life.
2. I have the *right* not to have to prove that I am in pain.
3. I have the *right* to control decisions regarding my pain.
4. I have the *right* to demand appropriate medical attention.
5. I have the *right* to be alone when I choose.
6. I have the *right* to refuse requests that may increase my pain.
7. I have the *right* to pain relief.

To all of you who have not yet found success in your search for pain relief or who have not been able to afford the search itself, I present, for your private use, THE SCOTTSDALE PAIN RELIEF PROGRAM.

Once you have completed the seven-day regimen and you are into your Lifetime Maintenance Program, you will realize that THE SCOTTSDALE PAIN RELIEF PROGRAM has become a part of your life—a life that is no longer controlled by pain.

Dr. Neal H. Olshan

THE SCOTTSDALE PAIN RELIEF PROGRAM

The Revolutionary Seven Day
Drug-Free Program to Reduce Pain

Dr. Neal H. Olshan

IVY BOOKS • NEW YORK

Ivy Books
Published by Ballantine Books
Copyright © 1987 by Neal H. Olshan

Library of Congress Catalog Card Number: 87-1103

ISBN-0-8041-0262-7

This edition published by arrangement with Beaufort Books Inc.

Manufactured in the United States of America

First Ballantine Books Edition: June 1988

To all people who suffer from pain

Contents

Part Two

Contents

Part Three

Acknowledgments

"Thank you" is a phrase that barely scratches the surface when I think of all the people who helped the Scottsdale Pain Relief Program become a reality.

I am indebted to my wife, Mary, who provided constant support and critical insights during long hours of writing. Her ability to analyze and suggest alternatives was magnificent.

I am also indebted to Sandy Olshan for her emotional support: "How's it going, Dad? You're doing really good!" To Bob Olshan for his humor and art work. A citation goes to Maureen Olshan for her constant support although she was sometimes uncertain why I was writing until 2:00 A.M. and up at 6:00 A.M.

A special thanks to Andrew Wolin, M.D. and Lynda Wolin, R.N. for sharing their medical knowledge, giving support, and providing many moments of laughter.

A warm and special thanks to my publisher at Beaufort, Susan Suffes, whose expertise and professionalism were invaluable. She is the publisher all writers hope to work with but seldom meet.

Preface

Have you ever wondered how many people actually read the introduction to a book? I hope you won't skip this introduction because I have some very important items to discuss with you before you begin chapter one.

Prior to beginning the Scottsdale Pain Relief Program, you should have consulted with a physician regarding your pain problem. *Never* proceed with the Scottsdale Pain Relief Program for an undiagnosed pain. As an example, a person experiencing headaches never should begin this program unless he or she has been examined by a physician. The Scottsdale Pain Relief Program has been designed to be compatible with any ongoing treatment and should not be used as a substitute for appropriate medical care.

Most of you who suffer from chronic pain have either been on a medication merry-go-round or are still going in circles with a seemingly endless progression of pills for your pain. Because there are so many different types of pain medication, you will need to consult with your physician about an appropriate program for reducing your medication intake in the safest manner possible. If you are presently taking medication, do not feel that you have to stop all medication prior to the seven-day program. Your success at controlling pain once you have completed the seven-day program and begun the Lifetime Maintenance Program should increase your pain tolerance and decrease your discomfort to a level that will allow you to substitute your personalized pain relief formula for medication. It is important to remember that you should never stop your medication abruptly or reduce medication without your physician's supervision.

As you will learn in chapter one, I have experienced chronic pain, and thirteen years ago, out of my own discomfort, I began development of what is now the Scottsdale Pain Relief Program. Although I would like to, I cannot guarantee you total pain relief; but if you follow the seven-day program and use the Lifetime Maintenance Program, you will gain control over your pain.

There are no complicated instructions or special skills needed as you enter and progress through the seven-day program. The development of your personalized pain relief formula will be through your input.

Once you have learned your personalized pain relief formula and through practice can apply it to your daily life circumstances, then you will begin to reclaim all those parts of your life that have been taken from you by pain.

Throughout this book I will serve as an adviser and gatekeeper. The true measure of success will be based upon your commitment, dedication, and willingness to learn a new technique to control pain.

Once you have completed the seven-day program and are into your Lifetime Maintenance Program, then you will realize that the Scottsdale Pain Relief Program has become part of your life—a life that is no longer controlled by pain.

For all of you who have not yet found success in your search for pain relief or have not been able to afford to go on a search for pain programs, I present to you, for your private use, the Scottsdale Pain Relief Program.

Part One

Part one of the Scottsdale Pain Relief Program contains all of the information you need to begin the seven-day segment. As you read through chapters one, two, and three, don't hesitate to take as much time as possible, rereading when necessary. Having the proper information and understanding is essential to the success of the seven-day program and ultimately your continued progress through the Lifetime Maintenance Program.

Throughout the first three chapters I have provided you with quotes from people who have completed the Scottsdale Pain Relief Program—people like you who suffer from pain. I have inserted these quotes because I feel that it will be more significant for you to hear from other pain sufferers rather than from pain "experts." Statements made by people just like you may help you to understand better the commitment and understanding needed for successful completion of the program.

Chapter One

A Beginning and a Solution

Take a moment to answer these questions:

Do you have pain for more than thirty minutes at least three times a week?

Does pain control part of your life?

Have you been unsuccessful in the search for pain relief?

If you have answered yes to any of these questions, then you need the Scottsdale Pain Relief Program. In seven days, you will begin to take control of your pain.

The Scottsdale Pain Relief Program has been designed to provide help to anyone who is willing to commit his or her time and effort to completion of the seven-day program and daily use of the Lifetime Maintenance Program.

A Book for You

I have developed and written this book for only one purpose: to help you learn how to relieve *your* pain. Even the design and style of the book is for you. Notice the book isn't heavy, the type is easy to read, and explanations are nontechnical and straightforward. People with neck, shoulder, or arthritis pain shouldn't have to hold a heavy, cumbersome book that could actually cause an increase in their discomfort.

If you are experiencing pain right now, and I would assume, if you are reading my book, you are hurting, there is little need to force-feed you chapter after chapter of research studies, scientific mumbo jumbo, quotes from "leading authorities," and explanations that end in the statement, "Unfortunately you are going to have to live with the pain." That's not much of an alternative!

You want help and you want it right now—that's what the Scottsdale Pain Relief Program is all about: to show you how to reduce your pain.

Types of Pain.

Below is a list of pain problems that have been treated with the Scottsdale Pain Relief Program.

Arthritis   Causalgia
Backaches   Cluster Headaches
Burns   Crohn's Disease
Cancer   Dental Work

Diabetic Neuropathy
Herpes
Irritable Bowel
  Syndrome
Menstrual Cramps
Migraine Headaches
Muscular Aches
Neuromas
Neural Pain
Phantom Limbs
Postsurgical Discomfort
Raynaud's Disease

Sciatica
Sinus Headaches
Sports Injuries
Sympathetic Dystrophy
Temporomandibular Joint
Syndrome (TMJ)
Tendinitis
Tennis Elbow
Tension Headaches
Tic Douloureux
Ulcerative Colitis
Ulcers

The Scottsdale Pain Relief Program has been success-fully providing help to pain sufferers for over five years. Now you can have the complete program.

It's yours for the rest of your life!

Your Beginning

The mere fact that you are reading this book means that you have at least the initial desire to seek a solution to a pain problem. The answer doesn't lie in the thousands of research papers, studies, and clinical textbooks. The solution to pain lies within each and every one of you. No one has ever taken the time to teach you the skills needed to activate the process that lies within all of us to gain control over our pain and thus begin

living life rather than just existing from day to day.

My Start

For over thirteen years I have read all the studies and research papers and attended panel discussions with doctors, clergy, scientists, and people who suffer from chronic pain. As a program consultant for the Commission on Accreditation of Rehabilitation Facilities, I have journeyed to all parts of the United States with teams of professionals evaluating and accrediting inpatient and outpatient pain centers, which can now be found in most major cities. I have also developed major pain programs for outpatients and hospitals. At present, I treat and work with pain patients every day of the week. Through the sum total of my thirteen-plus years, I have been drawn inevitably to this point, where I hope to provide you with the means by which to take control of your pain, no matter who you are, where you live, or what type of suffering you experience.

> *"How can you keep treating pain patients?"*

> *"Don't you get tired of hearing them complain?"*

> *"I would have burned out years ago."*

These are all comments I have heard over the years. I admit to being discouraged and frustrated at times not to be able to help a greater number of people. Very seldom does a week go by that I do not receive letters from people, some living as far away as Puerto Rico, pleading for some type of help. These people have read about my program in articles, heard me on the radio, or seen me talk on television programs trying to present the idea of hope for the chronic pain sufferer through the Scottsdale Pain Relief Program. For most, the cost of coming to Arizona for treatment is prohibitive. Prior to writing the Scottsdale Pain Relief Program, I could only provide encouragement and hope that they would find help wherever they were. Frequently I would receive additional letters months later detailing their own frustration in seeking appropriate answers and alternatives.

Facts and Figures

Nearly every book on pain seems obsessively weighted with facts and figures. Granted, a large, continually growing segment of our population suffers from pain on a minute-by-minute, hour-by-hour, and day-to-day basis; but other than letting you know that you are not alone, facts and figures do little to help you relieve discomfort. They might even push you to increased frustration. Obviously, all of these enormous numbers of people experiencing pain get little solace in reviewing the latest statistics from various state and governmental agencies—in case you haven't heard, we're dealing with an epidemic, one that enslaves greater numbers of people each and every day, with no visible end in sight.

The Numbers, Please

I have always found it interesting and slightly amusing that the first thing I am usually asked on television talk shows is to recite the pain "numbers." There seems to be definite shock value in pain's daily toll. Here are some of the annual figures: one-hundred and fifty million-plus people in the United States suffer from pain, twenty-one million people visit doctors for back pain, fourteen million hours of doctors' time is spent on treating headaches, and there are seventy-five million arthritis sufferers, forty-two million people experiencing headaches, and over one hundred million dollars a year spent in the United States for pain medication, salves, ointments, and other over-the-counter products. Besides letting you know you are not alone, they do little to help you feel better.

The Beginnings of My Pain

I am a chronic pain sufferer, one of the statistics!

That's right, I suffer from chronic back discomfort. For years I had back pain due to a football injury in college, but by applying to myself the principles I now teach daily to others, I have been able to reduce what had been an often distressing and disabling pain to a dull ache, which at times I don't even notice.

Because I know what it's like to experience the unrelenting, throbbing, searing, pinching, stabbing pain day after day, I can easily identify with others who experience pain. I am cautious, however, never to make that fatal mistake, when talking to a patient, of saying in a very authoritative tone, "I know just how you feel."

No one knows exactly how you feel because pain affects

each one of us differently. We can make certain assumptions about how someone in pain may feel, and we may draw parallels to other people we know or even ourselves, but you are the only one who truly knows what your pain is like, and what it has done to your life in the past, and what it is doing to your life now.

Most people who come to me for treatment are surprised to find that I have back "discomfort." When they come into my office, they may notice that the couch and chairs are firmer than usual and allow people to sit down and get up more easily without sinking into soft cushions. There are special pillows for back support. There is room in my office to stand up, stretch, and move about after sitting for long periods. The small pillow that I slip behind the base of my back when I sit down may be the first clue. I also get up and stretch or move every fifteen to twenty minutes.

I know what it's like to have wondered if tomorrow could be any worse. That was before I started searching for answers.

My Search

It's more the rule, rather than the exception, that people who come into my office are curious to know about my back pain. They are unaccustomed to meeting health care providers who are also chronic pain sufferers. I usually know they are wondering how it began for me.

As a second-string linebacker my playing time was usually limited to big wins or disastrous losses. During one of my shining moments I was blocked illegally. The pain was immediate, but I said nothing then for it was my chance to prove my worth as a football player. I continued to ignore the injury so that I could keep playing.

While in graduate school, I could stand it no longer. The pain was getting worse. It was difficult for me to sit for longer than twenty minutes without gritting my teeth. I went to neurologists, neurosurgeons, and orthopedic surgeons, who suggested various procedures from myelography (injecting special dye directly into the space around the spinal cord, followed by X rays which can reveal protruding disk matter) to laminectomies (surgery to remove the posterior arch of a vertebra). Medication was becoming a dark alley with no way out. It if was strong enough to deaden the pain, then I couldn't function in school. I was at Arizona State University studying psychology, and I felt there must be some other alternative rather than invasive (going inside the body) procedures or the medication merry-go-round.

I began to study pain and pain treatment, searching for answers. From those days at Arizona State University in the early 1970s, I knew that my professional and personal focus would be helping people who suffer from pain syndromes by developing new types of treatment.

Research, studies, and interviews all gave me the foundation of knowledge needed to gain a thorough understanding of the mechanisms involved in the pain response. I also learned that for every possible answer there were two or three unanswered questions that seemed to repeat year after year, with no one providing solutions.

The repeated questions involved the people who were not candidates for surgery whose medication wasn't working; or when they took enough to dull the pain, they could not function in any normal lifestyle setting. There was also the ever-enlarging group of people who had experienced failed surgeries. The common denominator among all these people, myself included, was the costly, time-consuming disappointment-after-disappointment "highway" we were instructed to follow to search for *someone* to take away our pain and suffering. I tried that route for five years with no results.

Finally, when I decided to get off the highway and search out an alternative, pieces began to fall into place. The answer seemed almost too simple: Develop a plan to teach people to control pain by using the body's built-in painkillers and at the same time help them to regain control of their lives.

I developed my first pain program in Scottsdale, Arizona, in 1975 at the first outpatient pain treatment center in the United States. Since that time, pain treatment centers have grown up faster than a group of well-fed bunny rabbits. Of course, along with the growth of pain treatment centers has been the appearance of pain experts. There are many scientists who are dedicated, hardworking professionals seeking answers to chronic pain, but, unfortunately, pain treatment has become a big-dollar item in the United States, with hospitals and clinics rushing to reap the burgeoning profits. As I worked into the late 1970s trying to develop and refine a workable pain program, I couldn't help but notice that every hospital of any size and stature had to have a pain program. These pain programs were usually four to six weeks in length and were inpatient (the person stayed in the hospital at least five days per week). During the course of treatment an individual would receive physical therapy, occupational therapy, recreational therapy, psychotherapy, biofeedback, and more. Usually these programs operated in a group format with anywhere from six to twelve pain patients being treated at a time. Costs ranged from 8000 to 18,000 dollars. The comprehensive programs were difficult to participate in for anyone who was employed either full or part time. Formats differed from program to program, but basically were multidisciplinary (a combined, coordinated thrust of numerous professionals). Some were good, some bad, and some just took the money and kept running.

In the early 1980s, the insurance industry suddenly awakened to the problem of pain treatment, panicked, and immediately began to place restrictions on reimbursement for pain treatment or pain management therapy. I found it quite astonishing, when interviewing several top executives of the major medical insurance companies, to be told candidly that they could not recognize pain as a problem that was amenable to treatment other than traditional (surgical, medication), because the cost to them would be phenomenal. At my first pain center I went head to head with insurance companies on more than one occasion. It was also frustrating to try to convince fellow members of the psychological and medical community that pain could be treated with alternatives to medication, prolonged physical therapy, or surgery.

Since I was experiencing pain, I had the opportunity to test all of my techniques on myself. Some worked, others held promise, and some were never to be tried again. I found that year after year my efforts seemed to focus more toward the body/mind connection and the brain's ability to develop systems to reduce and control discomfort along with the depression, anger, frustration, decreased self-confidence and irritability that all too often go hand in hand with pain.

The Scottsdale Pain Relief Program has been nearly ten years in development and implementation. What I present to you now is a program which may help you:

decrease pain

increase pain tolerance

increase self-confidence

reduce depression

reduce anxiety

regain control of your life

The Scottsdale Pain Relief Program is not a cure, and it is not a miracle. It is a very straightforward, honest, and reliable approach to gaining control of your pain. There are no shortcuts, magic pills, silver bullets, or enchanted wands—only application, dedication, and the true desire to be a victor in your daily battle against pain.

Chapter Two

Getting Started

Take a deep breath in through your mouth, exhale slowly through your nose, and let your shoulders relax . . . release the tension . . . and let's go.

As with all things, there must be a beginning, and so we find ourselves in the starting block of a long-distance race: the Pain Relief Marathon. To qualify for this event, you must first be willing to look at your circumstances and reactions to pain in an honest and open manner. Take a few moments now and complete the form that I have developed for you.

This will be the first questionnaire presented to you in the book. The directions will be relatively similar for each:

1. Answer all the questions based on how you have felt during the past ten days.

2. Don't seek help from anyone else to answer the questions.

3. If the statement does not apply leave it blank.

4. If you don't want to mark in the book, then number a blank sheet of paper from one to ten for use as an answer sheet.

5. Answer each question with yes or no.

Chronic Pain Qualifier

1. My pain has been present for more than four months.

2. I have been to at least two doctors for my pain condition.

3. I feel frustrated by my pain.

4. I am in pain at least fifty percent of my waking hours.

5. Sometimes, people don't understand my pain.

6. I feel as though the pain is controlling or beginning to control my life.

7. When my pain increases I become depressed and/or anxious.

8. I feel trapped by my pain.

9. Thinking about the future makes me nervous.

10. I am afraid the pain will increase.

If you have answered yes to five or more of these statements, then the pain is beginning to take control of your life, and the Scottsdale Pain Relief Program may be the answer you have been seeking.

Gaining Control

The story of Jim B. is sad and the all-too-often repeated testimony of the chronic pain sufferer. Jim suffered a back injury that eventually led to twenty-four years of nearly constant suffering. He has had a total of seven back surgeries. He has been addicted to pain medication (at one time as many as twenty Percodan per day). He has been treated over and over again with physical therapy and even has had age regression treatment supposedly taking him back to the time of his birth trauma.

When all of these treatments and therapies failed, leaving Jim a pain medication "junkie," he tried to commit suicide on two occasions. On the final suicide attempt, Jim sat in a bathtub with slashed wrists and ankles, watching his life's blood flowing down the drain. A doctor who realized he could help Jim no more recommended Jim see me for evaluation.

Jim completed the Scottsdale Pain Relief Program one-and-a-half years ago and now works every day at his Lifetime Maintenance Program. His battle remains a constant one, day in and day out. He strives to maintain control over the relentless pain.

This summer I received a card from Jim as he and his wife drove from Arizona to Minnesota.

Hi, Neal:

Had a good trip up to Minnesota. Staying with friends right on a huge lake—Fishing every day—boy—this is the life! Feeling just great—no pain! Praise the Lord! Thanks for making all this possible!

Jimmy

Jim, like so many others, regained control of his life.

False Expectations

The control of pain brings us to a very key issue. Many of you will have some discomfort for the rest of your life because of arthritis, injuries from accidents, or numerous degenerative types of diseases. Control *does not* imply an absence of pain. Although some people who use the Scottsdale Pain Relief Program will be able to completely short-circuit muscle contraction headaches, certain types of neuromuscular pain, and other pain conditions, the majority of you will have some residual discomfort. It should be so minimal, however, that it won't interfere with your life on a physical, emotional, social, occupational, educational, or personal level. Once you gain control, you need to maintain it on a consistent basis. You cannot experience a success and then turn away and expend no further effort. Because your efforts need to continue, I have included the Lifetime Maintenance Program.

Proof of Pain

I am going to ask you to do something from now on which may be difficult at first but is essential for your successful completion of the program.

From this moment on you do not have to prove your pain to anyone!

I know this may be difficult, since anyone with a chronic pain problem experiences the trauma of pain proof.

How many of you have experienced a referral merry-go-round as you go from one doctor to the next and ultimately find yourself sitting in the psychologist or psychiatrist's waiting room, fully convinced (if not brainwashed) into believing that the pain may be a figment of your imagination? Obviously, the pain is a response to an inadequate childhood, some frustration with your job, an unhappy sex life, or all of the above. By the second or third doctor, you want to set a tape recorder on the desk and play back the information you have provided to everyone else. Meanwhile your anger builds inside, festering with a resentment nurtured in your belief that no one fully understands your pain and suffering.

Over the years there have been times when I have actually had to deprogram people to help them regain confidence in their own belief system, convincing them that pain proof is not essential to pain relief.

In the past five years the medical community has made positive steps toward identifying and appropriately diagnosing pain conditions. Medical schools are finally realizing that the answer to pain is not a traditional doctor standing with a scalpel in one hand and a prescription pad in the other. Old traditions and institutions die hard, and unfortunately there are still too many medical personnel who will sit behind a large, protective desk, look over at a pain sufferer, and utter the infamous words, "You'll have to learn to live with it." You are then overcome with feelings of hopelessness and the belief that you have failed to prove your pain.

Friends and relatives are not exempt from this ordeal of proof. When nearly three-quarters of all pain sufferers find their marriages near or into divorce, they can usually look back to a spouse who really did not believe their pain.

The Proof Trap

When you allow yourself to be caught in the trap of proving your pain, the *what-if* statements follow:

> *"What if I were lying in a hospital bed with tubes sticking out of my body?"*

> *"What if my arm were in a cast?"*

> *"What if I had scars all over my face?"*

> *"What if I were dead?"*

> *"What if . . . ?"*

Along with the *what-if* statements are the projections, which sound like this:

"I wish my doctor could experience my pain for one day."

"I wish my family knew how bad my head hurt."

"I wish there were a way to measure the amount of pain I am in."

"I wish I were dead!"

The *what-if* and *I-wish* statements are all traps into which pain patients fall. All of us have at one time or another succumbed to some of these statements, which we utter in our own subconscious attempts at trying to prove that we are not imagining the pain but truly hurting.

Bill of Rights

Before you read this next section, I want you to get up from wherever you are sitting or lying and go to where there is a mirror. Stand or sit in front of that mirror, and as you read the Bill of Rights for People in Pain, I want you to stop after each sentence, look directly into the mirror, and repeat the sentence back to yourself five times. Each morning of the seven-day program, you are to repeat the bill of rights in front of the mirror, in the same manner, before you start your day. As you progress through the Scottsdale Pain Relief Program, you will learn to believe and trust in each of these statements. They will become *your* bill of rights, which you will earn through successful completion of the seven-day program and continued use of the Lifetime Maintenance Program. Like a bill of rights for any country or organization, they are only as potent as the people using them.

Over the years I have found that people who gain the most success from the program use and believe in their rights. To assert these rights in all situations is a matter of belief in yourself and your ability to control pain. Many people have taken these simple sentences and written them down on a piece of paper or a card to carry the bill of rights with them wherever they go. The card serves as a constant reminder and reinforcer.

The Bill of Rights for People in Pain

1. I have the *Right* to live a full and happy life.

2. I have the *Right* not to have to prove my pain.

3. I have the *Right* to control decisions regarding my pain.

4. I have the *Right* to demand appropriate medical attention.

5. I have the *Right* to be alone when I choose.

6. I have the *Right* to refuse requests that may increase my pain.

7. I have the *Right* to pain relief.

These rights are not to be taken lightly. They serve as the foundation for your Scottsdale Pain Relief Program and everything you build upon it through the Lifetime Maintenance Program.

The Emotional Side of Pain

Anyone who suffers from pain knows firsthand that pain can definitely affect your emotions. During the course of my practice I have always been amazed when people come into my office and talk about a pain condition they have had for three, five, or more years and then in the same breath tell me the pain has not in the least bit affected them emotionally or psychologically. We are not talking about pain that is psychogenic or caused by emotions but chronic pain, which inevitably leads to emotional fallout.

Admitting to yourself that the pain may be affecting you from an emotional standpoint can be the most difficult task. None of us likes to admit that we have emotional difficulties, especially when pain has already restricted our ability to enjoy life, maintain relationships, or work.

Emotional Fallout—A Closer Look

Take a few minutes and read through the descriptions of emotional difficulties that may be caused by pain. The number of problems and degree of severity may vary from person to person and are dependent upon type of pain, lifestyle, and basic personality structure.

Irritability.

"I can't be bothered with that now."

"Leave me alone and let me rest."

"Go ask your mother [father]."

Most people who suffer from a pain condition will recognize these statements. It is only natural that when you are in pain you will be more irritable. Noises, activities, conflicts, or even making decisions, which before the pain had presented little difficulty, now take major efforts and may cause you to feel on edge most of the time.

Depression.

"I don't have the energy."

"I just don't feel like doing anything."

"I just don't seem to be interested in anything."

Over the years depression has been given a connotation of severe mental illness, hospitalization, drug treatments, or electroshock therapy. There is no question that pain is depressing. It causes you to feel down, listless, and lacking energy. The longer the pain continues, the greater the possibility that depression will become a way of functioning and eventually a destructive coping mechanism. The essence of depression is nonactivity, and the factor of feeling sorry for yourself is a natural ingredient.

Increased Frustration.

"I don't have the patience anymore!"

"When is this going to end?"

"Why doesn't anyone listen to me?"

These statements are often made by pain sufferers. They are a direct result of the pain relief search ending in a blind alley. They are also found in the medication merry-go-round.

Anxiety.

"I feel jumpy all over."

"I feel shaky."

"I'm so nervous I can't think straight most of the time."

We are not talking about the anxiety that may be stereotyped on television or in movies. The anxiety that you experience with pain relates to how other people view you, whether they believe that you are in as much pain as you say, or your fear of what may happen in the future. When you look to the future, you wonder if it will be one where you are not constantly harassed by your pain. If the future looks bleak and your anxiety increases, then this creates what we call anticipatory anxiety. You are anticipating continuing pain fallout, and this creates a sense of anxiety, uneasiness, and shakiness, which may occur on a constant, once-daily, or even hourly basis. Worry about future pain long enough and you'll live in a constant state of anticipatory anxiety.

Anger.

"I feel like beating my head against the wall!"

"I just want to scream!"

"I want to hit someone or something."

These are statements made by people who are angry—angry at the fact that they have to continue suffering from pain. They are upset at how the pain has restricted their lives either at home or at work. The anger may eat away at you in the same manner that a cancerous malignancy can gradually steal your life. Many times irritability, frustration, and anger go hand in hand and appear to be partners in a conspiracy to cause you increased discomfort beyond the pain.

Hopelessness/Helplessness.

"I feel like giving up."

"I feel doomed!"

"What's the use?"

I've heard these statements over and over again from patients in my office. You may have heard them from friends or relatives, or possibly even yourself. The feelings of hopelessness/helplessness are generated as an outcome of any prolonged amount of pain. I talk to people every day who continually use the phrase, "I don't feel as though I have any control over my life with the pain." When there seems to be no solution to the pain, and day after day you suffer, then the feelings of hopelessness/helplessness begin to take seed.

Isolation.

"Just leave me alone."

"I just don't feel like going out of the house."

"No one understands how I feel."

You hurt both physically and emotionally. You begin to notice a lack of interest in being around people. Friends who normally called or came to visit seem to contact you less frequently. Even at work, you tend to isolate yourself from your coworkers, and they may ask you if something is wrong. Of course, there is the pain, but how do you tell them that you just don't feel like being around people?

Decreased Concentration.

"I read a page and then I can't remember what I have read."

"I can't seem to get into my work anymore."

"I keep asking people to repeat what they've told me."

People who suffer from headaches know full well the impact of their pain on the ability to concentrate and perform tasks that require them to focus their attention. A decrease in the ability to concentrate is not limited just to headaches but can affect you with any type of pain. The pain constantly interrupts your conscious focusing and is a negative distraction.

To Be Depressed or Not to Be Depressed?

That is the question. You are the only one with the answer. The pain-depression cycle is something you are going to overcome through the seven-day program. That sense of feeling down, blue, and fatigued can be alleviated through two steps:

1. Activation of the body's chemicals that are built-in antidepressants

2. Lifestyle changes that will halt the growth of depression and put you back in control of your emotions

The Pain-Depression Roller Coaster.

Some years ago a young woman sat in my office sobbing. She described her life as a mess. Two years before she had been rear-ended in an automobile accident and suffered a neck injury. No bones were broken, but the diagnosis had been severe cervical strain. Following her accident, her family doctor put her on muscle relaxants and pain medication. One month later she felt no better and in fact was now developing daily headaches. Her job performance was beginning to suffer because of the amount of time off from work she needed, and her social life was almost nonexistent. This was only the start. For the next two years she went to nine doctors, physical therapy, and various clinics. Her fiancé broke off their engagement, and her employer of five years threatened to replace her because of days missed for treatment and doctors' visits.

Every day she forced herself out of bed and tried to complete the duties of her job as secretary/receptionist. The pain continued unabated, and she noticed feelings of worthlessness, frustration, and a general sense of hopelessness. Her long-standing friendships began to crumble. There were feelings of confusion and anger, which fed directly into a quickly sinking self-worth.

Two-and-a-half years after the accident, she was unemployed, living with her parents, and feeling as though life were not worth living. She not only had a chronic cervical pain syndrome, but she had also developed a depression that was slowly destroying her life.

She was on the pain-depression roller coaster, from which she felt there was no escape. She was certain that nothing could help.

Fortunately a friend of her mother's had been through the Scottsdale Pain Relief Program and suggested that the daughter come to see me.

After reviewing her case, it was obvious to me that all the professionals had focused on her pain, provided her only minimal relief, and then had branded her as a hysterical woman. As the doctors' reports followed her from one office to the next, she might have worn a red *H* (for hysterical) painted on her forehead signifying that she was not stable and exaggerated her symptoms.

Convincing her to begin the Scottsdale Pain Relief Program was a difficult task. Her faith in doctors had been shattered along with her confidence. She didn't believe she had within her the capabilities for learning to control her pain and restabilize herself emotionally.

She soon came to learn that there was within her a power to slow the roller coaster and allow her to jump off at an appropriate time.

Fortunately the woman I have just described is capable of using the Scottsdale Pain Relief Program. There are literally hundreds of thousands of people who do not know about the Scottsdale Relief Program. They continue to ride the roller coaster, with little or no hope of ever getting off.

Is There a Chronic Pain Personality?

The never-ending effort to classify and put everything in its own special little box has not omitted the person suffering from pain. As early as the seventeenth century, the physician Thomas Willis described diabetes as being caused by ''an ill-manner of living, sadness, long grief.'' Passivity, depression, stress, sadness, and prolonged grief have all become viewed as components of a diabetic personality.

We have heard of the Type A personality, which is characterized by tense, aggressive, and always-on-the-go people who might be more prone to heart attacks and ulcerative diseases. In fact, the Type A personality has been so well publicized that new branches of therapy have been developed that are specially devoted to treatment of this problem.

Irritable bowel syndrome, which can become a chronic pain condition, has been associated with women who are high achievers and self-demanding with perfectionist qualities. Of course, the irritable bowel syndrome is not solely the province of women; it may be experienced by men, although statistics indicate that more women are sufferers from this condition.

The individual with arthritis has often been described as having a personality that involves depression, repression, stress, and anxiety. Quite obviously, the arthritic personality contains many of the attributes we find in chronic stress conditions.

Through the course of my own practice, I have seen the effects of chronic stress and tense and anxious personalities as they relate to skin disorders.

The physiological factors involved in headaches have been well known for years. People who are tense, driven, and unable to relax may be subject to muscle contraction or migraine headaches.

I could go on and on, citing quotes from as early as 1701 to the present day, from studies being conducted in major hospitals and research facilities throughout the United States.

Is there a chronic pain personality? I don't believe that there is a box that everyone who suffers from chronic pain can be placed into, but I have found certain psychological and emotional characteristics that appear to be prevalent in people who suffer from chronic pain. Whether or not we become involved in a chicken-and-egg (which came first?) discussion is of little consequence. The item of major importance is the identification of any characteristics you may have that could adversely be affecting your ability to control the pain.

Here is a summary of characteristics that I have found in chronic pain sufferers. Go through the list and evaluate how many of them might apply to you. The Scottsdale Pain Relief Program has been designed to help you remove as many of these negative characteristics as possible.

Depression

Repression

Anxiety

Self-demanding behavior

Tension

Dependency

Hostility and Your Pain.

"I sometimes get so angry!"

"I wish I could hit someone!"

"If I could break something, I would probably feel better."

"I feel like I'm going to explode."

Hostility will not only increase your pain but will also cause a decrease in your body's ability to control the discomfort. The link between unresolved hostility and physical illness has been well defined by the scientific community. In a scientific study conducted in North Carolina, 250 medical students were given psychological testing to measure hostility. Those who received the highest scores showed five times the number of heart problems than did those medical students with low scores on the hostility scale.

I could go on and on, citing studies that show a direct connection between hostility and increased physical dysfunction even in terms of the body's own immune system.

People suffering from pain conditions who are hostile not only experience greater increases in pain but also do poorly in pain treatment, whether it be surgery, medication, or teaching the body to produce its own built-in painkillers. As the director of a pain center in a major hospital, day after day I would see patients for evaluation and possible participation in the pain treatment program. When an individual would sit across from me and react in a very angry, hostile, and belligerent manner, I could with almost one hundred percent certainty predict failure for this person unless the individual identified and was willing to resolve the hostility, which otherwise would prevent him from ever controlling his pain.

If you consider yourself an angry or hostile person or have been told by other people that you are, take a look at the suggestions. Don't be afraid to try them. Losing some of your anger and hostility can be a definite boost toward success in the Scottsdale Pain Relief Program.

Suggestions:

When you feel the anger building, take an extra exercise/activity segment, leave the scene of the possible argument, or take a walk.

When you feel the anger reaching a point of explosion, use the pain relief breathing, and then use the pain relief scan on page 129. With both of these techniques you can short-circuit the anger response and make a decision based upon the proper combination of intellect and emotion.

Avoiding Pain Traps.

You are an explorer seeking out the mythical cave in which the secrets to pain control may be found. As you begin this difficult journey, I must warn you of the traps and pitfalls that threaten to slow and stop you in your search.

Fortunately there are rules to follow that will increase your chances of entering the cave and learning the secrets. Some of the traps are slight and only temporary, yet some of the pitfalls are fatally deep.

Carefully follow each of these suggestions as you begin your journey, and you may be able to avoid the traps.

> *Don't make your pain the center of every conversation.*
>
> *Don't use your pain as an excuse to get out of recreational or work activities.*
>
> *Don't use your pain to gain sympathy.*
>
> *Don't exaggerate your pain to control or punish others.*

Since we are all human, there is little doubt that no one can avoid all pain traps, but with a careful, concerted effort you will be able to insure that any pitfalls are only ankle deep.

You already know some of the methods for avoiding the traps. The program will teach you the rest.

Help! Can Anyone Hear Me?

I have always found a curious phenomenon surrounding people who have chronic pain. It doesn't matter whether that pain is from arthritis, headache, or a low back injury. After a certain amount of time, people around you become somewhat deaf. You get a sense of them hearing you but not listening to you.

I have to assume that you are not a constant, nagging complainer but simply a person who suffers pain, which becomes evident through facial expressions, certain comments, or gestures. People ask you if everything is all right or you are uncomfortable. When you answer them for the first time there is curiosity; up to the eighth time, sympathy; and then, without warning, they start to become deaf.

You may have already noticed this phenomenon with your doctor. In your quest for a solution to the pain, I am confident that you have encountered medical care providers who listen to you but don't hear what you are saying. Fortunately there are changes evolving within the practice of medicine, and additional emphasis has been placed in medical schools, internships, and residencies that will help doctors not only to listen, but actually to hear what their patients are trying to tell them.

The selective deafness syndrome may also apply to relatives or friends who turn a deaf ear to your continuing problem. They don't know what to say or do, or how to react to your complaints of pain. They may feel inadequate to deal with your call for help and therefore try to pretend that the problem does not exist by refusing to hear it.

Experiencing selective deafness among friends, associates, or relatives can be devastating for someone experiencing chronic pain. Most of you have already experienced this to one degree or another, and the experience may have left you with a bitter taste in your mouth.

Helping People to Listen and Hear You

Here are some hints to help you overcome the problem of selective deafness:

1. When you talk, strive to maintain eye contact.

2. Slow your speech, applying appropriate pauses.

3. Keep your sentences shorter and allow for responses.

4. If you are going to talk to a physician, write down your questions or comments in advance, and go through them one by one to seek answers.

Putting an End to the Emotional Fallout

If pain is a black cloud hanging over your head and you're constantly being rained on by the emotional fallout, then it's time to move out from under the shadow of your pain. As you progress through the seven-day program and into the Lifetime Maintenance Program, you will be excited as each drop of the fallout begins to disappear.

The Two Faces of Pain Relief

Pain relief can be a two-sided coin. When pain has been with you for an extended period of time, you may have some confusion when you experience pain relief. Being aware of the ways you might react will help you to deal with success in the most appropriate manner.

Sometimes the Last to Know

"I am afraid of success."

"If I begin to change, everyone will expect a miracle."

"If my pain is lessened, then people may expect more of me."

"I am afraid to believe in my good days."

Would you believe me if I told you about some people, who—although their pain is destroying their life—have become so accustomed to the discomfort that the thought of being without pain is extremely frightening?

Remembering the last time you had a good day, a time, although brief, when the pain seemed to be less? Your excitement was soon sabotaged by the thought, "Don't allow yourself to hope, since the pain will probably be back tomorrow." So instead of enjoying your freedom from pain, you waited complaisantly for the return of your nemesis.

The False Positive

Some people don't become pessimistic when they experience pain relief—rather they blast off into the outer space of uncontrolled positivism.

"My pain is a lot less today so by tomorrow it will be gone forever!"

Of course, the crash comes when tomorrow their pain has returned, leaving them depressed and feeling cheated. When people become so blindly positive that they forget the nature of their pain process, then they become very vulnerable to disappointment, which leads to an extra heavy cloudburst of emotional fallout.

A Matter of Balance

As on a teeter-totter, there has to be a proper balance between the fear of pain relief on one side and blind positivism on the other.

Striking the proper balance is a matter of continual practice and adjustment. As your pain never remains static, so, too, your emotional fallout may vary from day to day or week to week. Upon completion of the seven-day program, you will have balance.

Defining Pain: Is It Chronic or Acute?

Acute.

You are hanging a picture on the wall and the hammer slips off the nail and impacts your thumb. There is an instantaneous response of pain as nerves are compressed in the area of your thumb by the head of the hammer, a signal is shot to the brain that is reinforced visually as you look at your injury. The signal in your brain has been interpreted as pain; within a matter of microseconds you feel the pain exploding in your thumb. After a grimace, or possibly some well-chosen words, you might continue hanging the picture, revert to childhood behavior and suck on your thumb while throwing a temper tantrum, or even choose the wisest course of action and soak it in a glass of ice water.

Whichever method you've chosen, unless there has been nerve damage or bone broken, your pain should decrease in a matter of hours, with some residual soreness perhaps lasting several days. A week following the episode, there should be almost no discomfort and the memory of the pain will probably only occur next time you have to hang a picture.

This is an example of an acute pain response. All of us experience acute pain responses almost every day of our lives, whenever we bump a knee on the edge of a table or stub a toe.

A Tale of Chronic Pain.

Let's move past your sore thumb, which of course no longer bothers you since it has been a week since your picture-hanging incident. It's Monday morning and you're at work, minding your own business, when Harry asks you to help him move the copy machine to the other side of the room. He assures you that between the two of you, it will be a snap. Well, it does turn out to be quite a snap because as you bend over and begin lifting your corner of the machine, Harry decides to look at the new office assistant as she walks by and shifts the weight of the machine to your side. You're in a bent-over position with your legs straight. As you struggle to catch the machine, there is a searing pain that shoots across your low back. Gritting your teeth, you struggle to maintain balance while Harry senses your predicament and regains his share of the load. The copy machine is now moved, but you spend the rest of the day taking aspirin and walking as though you're still trying to lift the copier. You tell yourself that the pain will soon disappear and that all you did was stress your back.

The day after the copy machine incident, the development of chronic pain begins. If you were to write a diary, here's how it would look:

Day after went to family doctor—painkillers and muscle relaxants—stay home rest of the week.

Four days later—not any better—called doctor, who said to come in.

Saw family doctor—he seemed perplexed but gave me

some medication to help me sleep better and told me to continue taking the muscle relaxants and pain pills.

Went back to work but by eleven o'clock in the morning the pain was in my back and left leg.

Called family doctor and he referred me to an orthopedic surgeon friend of his.

Could not get in for an appointment for four days.

Saw orthopedic surgeon, who took X rays and examined me—said I had low back strain and to take muscle relaxants—I told him that I was already taking muscle relaxants and he gave me a different kind—said to "take it easy on my back."

Now two weeks after hurting my back and it feels worse.

Becoming frustrated and angry.

Have not been able to play tennis since the injury.

Trying to work but it's hard to sit for long periods of time.

Went back to orthopedic surgeon and he prescribed different medication.

Heard about a physical medicine and rehabilitation doctor from a friend and made an appointment to see him.

Saw new doctor and was given new medication plus physical therapy five times a week.

Three months later, still going to physical therapy, now three times per week—job interrupted all of the time.

Have tried nine different kinds of medication.

Cannot sleep during the night.

Feeling depressed during the day.

. . . and on, and on, and on.

You have just witnessed the typical development of a chronic pain condition affecting the low back. This scenario is repeated with thousands of people each and every day to varying degrees as we become a population plagued by chronic pain problems.

You could probably write your own diary regarding your specific pain, whether it be headache, arthritis, or back pain.

Pain Anticipation.

Ask anyone who suffers from chronic pain, and they will tell you of their constant fear: "I wonder how I can live when the pain gets worse." Most pain sufferers live in dread of "the big one," with a constant level of anxiety and stress. Spending your time wondering and anticipating the next increase in pain sets the stage for pain anticipation.

An Unconscious Trigger.

If you consciously spend time focusing on the next attack you may have or an increase in pain due to other circumstances, then inadvertently you may be setting yourself up for "the big one." Focusing on the possibility of increased pain creates a chronic stress situation that serves as a trigger for increased muscle tension, muscle spasms, and decreased production of internal pain-controlling and emotion-stabilizing chemicals.

The triggering does not happen immediately, but given enough time and repetition of thoughts regarding a fear of pain increase a domino principle will take effect, triggering the increase in pain. When the pain does increase, the little voice inside you says, "See, I told you so." Once that little voice has spoken, the emotional dominoes (anxiety, depression, decreased self-image, decreased self-esteem) begin to fall.

Pain Pumpers.

Pain pumpers are behaviors or conditions that are directly under your control. The greater the number of pain pumpers, the more chance there will be of an increase in your pain and a possibility of sabotaging your efforts to control and reduce discomfort. See how many of the pumpers on the list are familiar to you, and use the Scottsdale Pain Relief Program to reduce as many as possible.

Stress
Anger
Anxiety
Overweight condition
Poor eating habits
Smoking (nicotine addiction)
Misuse of pain medication
Pain anticipation

Pain manipulation
Poor sleeping

Before You Start the Program

In chapter four you will actually begin the Scottsdale Pain Relief Program by preparing for the seven-day program. You may be surprised to learn that you have already progressed through very important aspects of the Scottsdale Pain Relief Program just by coming this far.

As chapter two ends, you need to become aware of the three types of people who start the Scottsdale Pain Relief Program. If you find yourself in any one or a combination of these types, then be honest enough with yourself to admit the fact and allow for any changes before day one.

Harry Have-A-Look.

Harry figures that he is going to take a look at the program. He doesn't want to commit himself at this point, but he plans to read through the seven-day program and see if it suits his needs. He has also made a decision that if he does not like the program, he can stop at any time he wants. The Harry Have-A-Looks need to make a definite commitment before even beginning the next chapter. If you have a habit of starting projects and never completing anything, then you may be a Harry. If you are, your first step will be to recognize the problem and make the commitment to start the seven-day program. Constantly be alert to the possibility of slipping back into the Harry Have-A-Look condition.

Mary Maybe.

Mary is similar to Harry Have-A-Look, but Mary usually completes whatever she begins, although never in a comprehensive manner. She is committed to completing what is started, but she tends to perform on only a superficial level. "Maybe it will work and maybe it won't" are her guiding words. Mary Maybe's need is to start the program with the conviction of obtaining success.

Jerry Joiner.

Jerry will join almost anything. He has been known always to complete applications that are addressed in the following manner: "You have been selected." Usually Jerry has heard about the Scottsdale Pain Relief Program from someone else or heard it mentioned on the radio or television. Jerry tends to buy the book and read the first several pages before putting it down on the coffee table and returning to his favorite television program—which will soon be interrupted by his chronic pain problem. If you're a Jerry, ask yourself if you have anything more important to do than spending seven days with a chance of gaining control over your pain.

Just One Minute: Before You Go Any Further

Before you proceed to chapter three, take this brief test, answering each question with a yes or no:

1. I have read chapters one and two completely.

2. I understand how the emotional fallout from pain may affect my life.

3. I am willing to go back and reread any areas that I don't thoroughly understand.

4. I am committed to continuing my search for relief from my pain.

5. I am beginning to feel there is hope.

If you have been able to answer yes to all of these questions, then it is time for you to move on to chapter three.

Part Two

If you are like most chronic pain sufferers, it has taken years to reach the point you are at today. All the frustration, misinformation, depression, anguish, and—most important—pain are going to be changed forever with your commitment to begin day one of the intensive seven-day program.

A Design for You.

By now you may have come to the realization that although I do not know you personally, it sounds and feels as if the Scottsdale Pain Relief Program was designed specifically with you in mind. It is my hope that you have this feeling, since the program was developed and modified through input, practice, and experimentation by people just like you.

Chapter Three

The Pain Segments

Pain Segment Particulars.

As you go through this section, normal curiosity will probably lead you to look at other segments besides the one for your specific pain. You will notice that some segments are not very large while others encompass numerous pages. This is not to say that one pain problem is greater than another; it only indicates that certain pain conditions may affect a greater number of people in our population.

Crossover.

After reading your pain segment, you should look at other types of pain and suggestions that have been provided. There is a significant crossover effect; for example, certain suggestions found in the back pain segment regarding posture and sitting can be and should be applied by everyone whether or not they have a back injury. In fact, I encourage every patient who goes through the Scottsdale Pain Relief Program to read the other pain segments and utilize the suggestions as a preventative medicine technique. Performing some of the exercises found in the back segment will help you to prevent future back difficulties, and you will benefit from overall neuromuscular fitness (flexibility, endurance, and strength). Don't be afraid to cross over.

Using the Pain Segments.

The pain segments should be referred to for your specific type of pain or condition. Each pain segment will describe briefly the type of pain and present helpful suggestions, which may include:

Exercises
Alternative treatments
Activities: do's and don't's

Your specific pain segment should be read and thoroughly reviewed prior to your beginning the seven-day program.

The Pain Relief Statement.

The pain relief statement is to be inserted into your personalized pain relief formula on day six of your seven-day program. The pain relief statement will serve as a mental trigger to activate further the body's built-in ability to reduce pain.

The Foundation.

The use of a pain relief statement is based on research with autogenic therapy (a method of self-control through repetition of body/mind phrases). In use since the early 1900s, autogenic therapy can be found at almost all major pain centers in the United States. My doctoral dissertation from Arizona State University was on the use of autogenic therapy for the treatment of anxiety and stress conditions. At the time I wrote my dissertation, there were over two thousand scientific articles worldwide relating to the benefits of autogenic therapy, and only twenty of these were in English. Times have changed, and since then autogenic therapy has been accepted universally as a technique for the following:

Anxiety reduction
Pain reduction
Increased body/mind interaction
Stabilization of emotional difficulties (anxiety, depression, phobias, etc.)

Autogenic therapy in its traditional format may take as long as from three to four months for full training and activation of the formulas. When I first began using autogenic therapy in the treatment of pain patients, I would follow the prescribed length of treatment but found it to be cumbersome, frustrating to the patient, and too long.

Over several years, I worked to modify the formulas without losing their inherently beneficial effects. Although the pain relief statements appear to be quite simple, within their basic nature lies their success. Unlike other treatments, pain relief statement utilization does not demand anything from your body/mind interaction; rather you make a passive, yet assertive, statement. If repeated in conjunction with your personalized pain relief formula, this statement will direct the appropriate body/mind interaction. Since you will be providing the statement to yourself, the control remains totally within you.

Repetition of the Statement.

When you are asked to repeat silently the pain relief statement (autogenically), you should bear in mind some very specific do's and don't's.

Do take your time

Do repeat the phrase silently in a rhythmic and paced manner

Do modify the statement to the extent of providing the best possible description of your condition or pain site

Don't force the statements

Don't modify the statement to make it a demand

Don't be fooled by the statement's simplicity and forget to include it as part of your personalized pain relief formula

Headaches

Wherever I go I ask the question, "What comes to mind when I mention the word *pain*?"

Eight out of ten times the response is:

HEADACHE!

The number of people suffering from headaches and the costs of this type of pain are staggering.

Headaches are the most common ailment in our country, affecting ninety percent of all Americans.

From ten to twenty percent of the American population suffers from recurrent migraine and cluster headaches.

More than forty-two million Americans are treated for headaches each year.

An estimated 126 million sick days are lost each year for headaches.

The cost to employers for sick days as a result of headaches is estimated at six billion dollars.

Less than ten percent of all headaches is caused by disease.

If you experience headaches, all of the statistics in the world are not going to make them go away or help decrease either the pain or how much it devastates your life.

Different Types and Causes.

Headache sufferers find little comfort in knowing that over forty-two million other Americans have frequent headaches and that seventy percent of all households have at least one person who is headache prone.

Most pop aspirins and comfort themselves with the knowledge that headaches, though painful, are not usually indicative of serious illness.

Whether you have a muscle contraction headache or a migraine headache, I am sure that well-meaning friends and physicians have all jumped at the opportunity to inform you of the latest cure or diet.

Why is it that a headache sufferer will eat a piece of chocolate and soon after develop a headache but several weeks later ingest the same amount of chocolate and experience no headache?

Why on one Friday night might you have four or five drinks and wake up the next morning with a horrible hangover but the next weekend repeat the same drinking and have no headache?

Both male and female bodies go through monthly cycles that determine whether or not you may get a headache. Women are more sensitive to headache food triggers around the time of their menstrual periods. Men have similar cycles, but these are harder to predict.

The body and mind work together to regulate body cycles. Dips and swings in the body's chemistry create either a friendly or a hostile ground for headaches to develop.

(Note: If you experience recurring headaches, you should have them evaluated by a qualified physician prior to beginning the Scottsdale Pain Relief Program to rule out their being the result of some ongoing disease process, such as tumors.)

This section will cover each of the major types of headaches: tension, migraine, cluster, and sinus. You probably already know which particular type you suffer from, but I've presented all of them. Before you go any further, just spend a few minutes and read through all the different types to make sure that what you think you have is what you really have.

Headaches in Review.

Each type of headache will have characteristics that are used to make a diagnosis. Some of these may be common to more than one type of headache. Read over the lists, especially the one for your headache. If you have been told that you have one particular type of headache but the description does not match up, then you should seek a consultation with a doctor specializing in the diagnosis and treatment of headache conditions.

Tension Headaches

Steady pain
Pain on both sides of head
Pain may last for days or weeks
Feels like band around head
Direct link to emotions (stress)
May occur day or night
May increase during the day

Migraine Headaches

Throbbing, recurrent pain
Usually on one side of head
May be felt around one eye
May have visual distortions (scotoma)
Increased irritability
Pallor
Dizziness
Sweating
Strange hearing and taste sensations
May occur without warning
Lasts from several hours to days
Nausea and possible vomiting
May have loss of speech or motor coordination
May start around menstrual period
May see glittering or scintillating forms
Sensitivity to light (photophobia)
Nose may run

Cluster Headaches

Little or no warning
May last from minutes to several hours
Usually last between thirty and ninety minutes
Flushing
Behind one eye
Tearing from affected eye
Nostril on affected side congested, may run
More common in males age twenty to forty

Sinus Headaches

Pain increases in head-down position
Dull, deep, pressure-like pain
Pain increases with bending or stooping
Pain starts above eyes
Pain may spread to forehead or cheeks
Nasal congestion
Gradually increases during the day
May follow infection
May occur seasonally (peak allergy times)

Stress and Your Headache

To Stop Before They Start.

You will soon be using the Scottsdale Pain Relief Program on a daily basis along with the pain relief statement. Your personalized pain relief formula should be used daily and whenever you feel the beginning of stress or tension. Don't wait until after you already have the headache.

Finding the Stress Around and Within You.

You're going to be a detective. As the famous stress sleuth, your job will be to search out all those parts of your environment that lead to a stress response and ultimately your headache. Now take a sheet of paper. On it list everything you can think of that causes stress in your life. Once you have made this list, take out a second sheet of paper and make two columns. In the first column list all the items you could possibly change that are within your control.

An example of such an item was found by Linda, who seemed to develop a headache every morning after her fourth-grade-level daughter had left for school. Linda identified the stress as the tension created trying to select her daughter's clothes in the morning amid the constant arguments about what she was going to wear. This was a stress within Linda's control. She had her daughter pick out the clothes the night before. Another example would be that of Richard, who found the traffic so congested on the way to work that by the time he sat at his desk, he had the beginning of a headache. Richard evaluated the stressor and when he found the traffic to be a major cause he planned an alternative, less congested route that would allow him to arrive at work early, less stressed.

Now take your list of stressors, and in the second column list all of the items that are not under your control to change. An example of something not under your control would be the condition of the street in the middle of your town, the Internal Revenue Service, or the dispostion of your boss.

Now develop a plan to reduce the stressors that are under your control. Do this slowly, picking first the easiest to change. Take your time as you slowly move through the list. Each item you remove adds increased control into the arsenal in your battle against the effect of stress on all types of headaches.

Your Pain Relief Statements

Your pain relief statement should be used on day six of the seven-day program.

Tension Headaches.

I am in control of my tension headache and stress.

Migraine Headaches.

I am in control of my migraine headaches and my hands are warm.

[Increasing hand warmth has been found to be an effective technique to short-circuit the beginning of a migraine headache.]

Cluster Headaches.

I am in control of my cluster headaches and stress.

Sinus Headaches.

I am in control of my sinus headaches and my forehead is pleasantly cool.

[The use of coolness has been shown to be effective in the reduction of pressure and swelling in sinus headaches.]

Back Pain

"Low back pain is the price we pay for upright posture," explains the neurosurgeon James Campbell of the Johns Hopkins Medical Institution in Baltimore. Gravity and the mechanics of the spine make low back pain commonplace: According to Dr. Campbell, an estimated eight out of ten people will have at least one significant episode of low back pain during their lifetimes.

There it is. You wake up in the morning and your back is so stiff, you can't even get out of bed. Maybe you bend over to pick up a piece of paper—and can't straighten up again. Your car is rear-ended, and several days later your back pain is beginning to drive you crazy.

On any given date, 2.4 million Americans are disabled by back trouble. That works out to approximately ninety-three million workdays lost each year.

A New Diagnosis.

During the course of my professional career treating pain, I have been aware of changes within the medical profession regarding how back pain is viewed. Surgical procedures appear now to be considered as a court of last resort. I have found doctors slightly more hesitant to begin treatment by immediately prescribing antiinflammatory or narcotic pain medication. The medical profession is definitely becoming aware of the role played in back pain by tension and stress. (The diagnosis of stress-caused back pain and stress-caused increase in the severity of a preexisting back condition is now being considered more thoroughly by doctors.) Doctors are becoming aware of the need for a method to break the back pain stress cycle.

Back Pain → Stress → Increased Muscle Tension →
Increased Pain → Increased Stress → Emotional
Fallout → Increased Pain → Increased Stress → and
on and on

The Scottsdale Pain Relief Program will be used to interrupt the pain stress cycle.

Three Major Causes: Sleeping, Sitting, and Standing on Your Back Pain

The Seat of the Problem.

What type of chair you sit in can play a very important role in your battle against pain. Although you may be using your pain relief imagery formulas on a daily basis and have just achieved excellent results from the seven-day program, your sitting in a chair that causes microscopic reinjuries to your back on a minute-to-minute basis will destroy much of the good work you have done.

If you have the type of job that requires you to sit for long periods of time, don't put off getting the proper chair. If your employer isn't convinced, then you may need to return to your physician and request a note or prescription from him specifying that you need a chair correct for your back.

Before you buy any chair for your personal or business use, consult the following recommendations:

A chair should provide correct support for the spine in every sitting position. To support the lower back and check the effect of the pelvis tilting forward, the bottom half of the back rest should have extra padding.

The top of the backrest should reach your shoulders so that it will support the spinal column.

The angle between the seat and the backrest should adjust automatically when you are either leaning forward working or leaning backward relaxing, as well as when you are sitting upright.

The seat height also should be adjustable, with the seat raised or lowered so that your feet rest comfortably on the floor. Look for a seat that slopes downward at the front edge and curves upward at the back. This feature, in conjunction with the backrest, insures proper back support. It also reduces pressure on the thighs, which insures adequate blood flow in the legs and feet and minimizes fatigue.

The chair's operating controls should be unobtrusive and easy to manipulate.

A good chair can be a definite asset in pain relief and your Lifetime Maintenance Program.

Standing Up to the Pain.

"I stand at my job all day as a checkout clerk, and I'm lucky if I can sit down during lunch."

"I'm on my feet all day at the post office and by ten-thirty in the morning, my back is already beginning to kill me."

"Standing at the sales counter for an eight-hour day leaves me with so much pain that when I get home in the evening, the only thing I can think about is lying down and not being bothered by my family."

If some of these statements ring true, then it is about time you took some steps to modify your standing behavior and begin to reduce the stress on your low back. Standing for prolonged periods of time fatigues the muscles in the hips, low back, and abdomen, which tends to pull the pelvis forward, causing strain on the low back muscles.

If you must stand for long periods of time, definitely try these suggestions:

Using a small stool, put one foot on the stool, alternating every few minutes. This technique will relieve some of the strain on the low back muscles, allow for better blood flow to the affected areas, and help return the spine to a more natural curve.

Don't stand in one position for prolonged periods of time, even if you only have a small space in which to work. Move every few minutes or so.

Don't be rigid. Flex your knees, and if possible do some minimal stretching movements several times every hour.

Putting Back Pain to Sleep.

The worst enemy of your back, guaranteed to leave you waking in the morning with increased pain, is a poor mattress. I know of very few doctors who, even though they know the importance of an appropriate mattress, will take the time to explain why having the right kind of mattress may not only prevent a continuation of your back pain, but may also aid in the overall healing process. Without the right kind of mattress, this prayer is usually repeated each night:

"Now I lay me down to sleep, my back pain I will surely keep."

For my back condition, I prefer a firm mattress. Many of my patients have found the waveless type of water bed to be excellent for a good night's sleep with a minimal amount of awakening discomfort. If you have difficulty obtaining a new mattress or a water bed, then a three-quarter-inch-thick piece of plywood inserted under your mattress may provide enough additional support.

Without the proper mattress, the following chain reaction will occur:

Back pain—poor mattress—poor sleep—increased fatigue—microreinjuries while sleeping—leads to increased pain, stiffness, and fatigue upon awakening.

Although the Scottsdale Pain Relief Program may be used with any type of mattress, why not take the time and get the best mattress for your particular back problem?

Sweet Dreams.

When you have back pain (or any other pain), getting a good night's sleep is difficult enough even without causing microscopic reinjury to your back when you are lying in bed. We have already discussed the need for an appropriate mattress or bed, but how you position yourself down to sleep makes a big difference to the way you are going to awaken in the morning.

"What's the big deal with how I sleep? I just lie down and finally the pain eases slightly and I fall asleep. So what's the big deal? I'll wake up in the morning feeling lousy anyway."

Comments like that have been made to me over and over. Again, we return to the basic concept that the Scottsdale Pain Relief Program will provide you with a method for using pain relief imagery to facilitate the body's production of built-in painkillers. You don't live in an isolated cocoon, though, and so you need to evaluate other aspects of your lifestyle based upon what type of pain you may suffer. If having the right type of bed or mattress possibly can reduce your overall discomfort by from one to one-and-a-half percent, and using the proper sleep position can further reduce this by another one percent, then before you know it, you have just decreased your pain by approximately from two-and-a-half to three percent. All these small bits help to reinforce the basic pain relief imagery and *do* add up to pain relief.

Here's how to sleep and allow your back to be in the best position for continued self-healing. (These suggestions may be used with any pain condition.)

Bend your knees, unlocking your spine into a neutral position, to relieve muscle and ligament stress.

Lie on your side with the hips and knees bent toward the chest and the head on the pillow.

Many times a small pillow between the knees will support the upper legs so circulation in the lower legs is not blocked.

A small pillow between the legs may prevent the lower back from twisting.

If you must lie on your back, then place a pillow under your knees to prevent a swayback position.

Do not use an extremely fluffy pillow.

Changing positions frequently while you sleep is not bad.

Now, have a good night's sleep.

The Best Little Back Exercises in the World.

Exercise, *stretch*, and *strengthen* are the key words for anyone with a bad back. Having a bad back has qualified me to try most of the exercises that seem to find their way into doctors' offices, magazines, and popular books devoted to the back. Everyone seems to have their own little special exercise that is guaranteed to help decrease back pain and prevent reinjury.

Total Agreement—Unbelievable.

Experts, including orthopedic surgeons, specialists in physical rehabilitation, neurologists, neurosurgeons, physical therapists, and exercise therapists, are in agreement about certain exercises that are essential for anyone experiencing back pain. Your physician should be able to provide you with the appropriate exercises for your condition.

Summary.

Coping with back pain is never a single-item endeavor. Exercise, proper diet, appropriate body weight, and your personalized pain relief formula will all help you to deal with it.

Your Pain Relief Statement

Your pain relief statement for back pain will contain an emotional component. Use the complete statement on day six.

I am in control of my back pain and stress.

Arthritis

What do the following people all have in common?

   Neanderthal man
   Alexander the Great
   Julius Caesar
   Henry VI
   Benvenuto Cellini
   Egyptian pharaohs

All of these people suffered from arthritis, along with over seventy-five million people in the United States.

Arthritis is basically an inflammatory process by which the body's own immune system turns against its host and begins to attack the body's own tissues.

There are over one hundred forms of arthritis, including rheumatoid arthritis, gout, systemic lupus erythematosus, osteoarthritis, ankylosing spondylitis, polymyositis, tennis elbow, and fibrositis.

In the United States, seventy-five million people experience arthritic-type symptoms in their joints and muscles on a repeated basis. Of the approximately one hundred types of arthritis currently known, there are eight major categories: synovitis, attachment arthritis, crystal arthritis, joint infection, cartilage degeneration, muscle inflammation, injury conditions, and other general conditions.

Synovitis.

This condition indicates that the lubricating fluid in our joints has become inflamed. The joint may feel warm or swollen and have red skin. Synovitis may occur at any age. It appears mostly to strike women. A more common name for synovitis is rheumatoid arthritis.

Attachment Arthritis.

Attachment arthritis causes the ligaments (which are attached to the bone) to become inflamed. Attachment arthritis appears mostly to affect men and appears usually between the ages of fifteen and forty. The condition is most commonly known as ankylosing spondylitis. It is sometimes referred to as *poker spine*.

Crystal Arthritis.

The most common form of crystal arthritis is gout. As the name implies, chemical crystals develop and are then found in the joint fluid. This condition may also be known as microcrystalline because the crystals formed in the joint space are very small. As with attachment arthritis, crystal arthritis appears mostly to affect men. It has an onset between the ages of thirty-five and ninety.

Joint Infection.

In this condition, bacteria invade the joint fluid and infections occur, which are commonly known as staphylococcus or gonococcus infections. This type of arthritis may affect any individual, at any age, and usually is treated effectively with antibiotics.

Cartilage Degeneration.

Whenever there is a breakdown in the joint cartilage the condition is known as osteoarthritis or osteoarthrosis. It may affect equally men or women, but it usually does not set in until after the age of forty-two. Due to the constant use of joints, which results in wear and tear over a period of time, this type of arthritis occurs in almost every individual, if the person lives long enough.

Muscle Inflammation.

As the name implies, this type of arthritis is found not in joints but in muscles. The muscle tissue becomes inflamed, causing pain and difficulty in movement. Muscle inflammation does not show any preference to sex or age. It is known more commonly as polymyalgia rheumatica, polymyositis, and dermatomyositis.

Injury Conditions.

This type of arthritis results from injury or irritation. It may be caused by back strain, tennis elbow, or shin splints.

Other Arthritic Conditions.

Systemic lupus erythematosus is considered a form of arthritis. At one time it had a mortality rate of from thirty to forty percent within five years. Development of new treatment techniques has reduced significantly the death rate, but the crippling effects continue. Additional conditions that are classified in the general category are: fibrositis and rheumatism associated with psychological conditions such as depression.

Summary.

There is no question that arthritis is a frightening, painful, crippling disease process that strikes a high number of our population. Many people with arthritis go on with their daily lives, but some suffer such severe crippling effects that they are bedridden and eventually become so disabled that they cannot care for themselves.

Your Pain Relief Statement

The pain relief statement for arthritis will include an emotion-stabilizing part. Insert the pain relief statement on day six.

I am in control of my _____ [pain site, pain condition] and my _____ [the word for the emotion or condition].

Example: I am in control of my hand pain and my depression.

Muscle Pain

The area of muscle pain contains probably the largest number of people suffering discomfort. Muscle pain can range from certain arthritic conditions to muscle damage caused by improper jogging shoes. Classified under muscle pain are the following categories: low back pain, neck pain, temporomandibular disorder joint dysfunction (TMJ), tension headaches, and various sports injuries.

You can see that the area of muscle pain is quite large. Actually there is some crossover between various conditions.

In this part of the chapter, I have tried to include some of the more prominent muscle pains, including symptoms. At the end of each description, I have provided you with the pain relief statement to be inserted on day six into your personalized pain relief formula.

If Yours Is Not Included.

If your specific muscle pain condition has not been included in this section, don't worry. You will still be able to insert this pain relief statement on day six.

I am in control of my _____ [insert pain site or pain condition] and _____ [response].

Example: I am in control of my shoulder pain and stress response.

Neural Pain

The category of neural pain describes conditions that directly affect the nerves of the body. Examples of neural pain are: trigeminal neuralgia, tic douloureux, postherpetic neuralgia, sympathetic dystrophy, neuromas, causalgia, and sciatica. All neural pain conditions involve damage, pressure, or inflammation that adversely affects the nerves and creates pain signals. The causes of neural pain may be viruses, trauma, infection, or damage to an associated structure. Whatever the cause may be, the pain is initiated directly by nerve damage. The pain may range from stabbing bursts to a constant burning sensation.

Trigeminal Neuralgia and Tic Douloureux.

Many times these two conditions are considered as one since they both affect the trigeminal nerve found in the face. The pain from these conditions can be excruciating. The discomfort may be constant or occur at intervals. For some people who suffer this type of neuralgia, the pain may be set off by vibration, air movement, or contact with the skin over the nerve.

Postherpetic Neuralgia.

Postherpetic neuralgia is a very painful condition resulting directly from the aftermath of herpes zoster. This is the same virus that causes chicken pox in children; but in adults, collagens may occur under the skin, damaging nerves. Although lesions on the skin may disappear, the nerve damage remains. Nerve fibers may be destroyed (mostly large nerve fibers), but damage to the smaller nerve fibers (those that carry pain messages) continues through the course of the disease.

Sympathetic Dystrophy.

Sympathetic dystrophy may be caused by trauma, surgery, or degenerative diseases. This condition is sometimes difficult to diagnose since the pain may not occur at the site of the original injury; for example, following a hand injury a person may develop a sympathetic dystrophy that causes constant pain in the arm, shoulder, and neck.

Neuromas.

Neuromas are globes (tumors) that form on nerve endings and lead to intense chronic pain. Whenever you have a nerve damaged by trauma, there is a possibility that a neuroma tumor will grow at the site of the injury. People who have nerves severed due to an accident may be more prone to forming neuromas. Some people have been shown to have a tendency toward neuroma growth.

Causalgia.

Causalgia is the general term used to describe various types of nerve damage where the pain occurs as a burning sensation.

Sciatica.

Sciatica has been associated with low back injuries. The pain is usually described as constant and going down the leg and ending in the foot. Sciatica usually increases with prolonged sitting, especially since the chair may press against the sciatic nerve in the back of the leg.

Summary.

From all the examples I have given to you, it is quite easy to see that neural pain accounts for a significant number of chronic pain syndromes. Neural pain may be combined with muscle pain to form a pain complex. Unfortunately, most cases of nerve damage will remain with an individual for the rest of his or her life. The Scottsdale Pain Relief Program's Lifetime Maintenance Program will be essential not only for initial pain relief but also for the possibility of continued pain relief in the future.

Your Pain Relief Statement

Your pain relief statement will be inserted on day six and is to be used with your personalized pain relief formula. Your statement should be as follows:

> I am in control of my _____ [pain control or pain site] and my [emotions].
> Example: I am in control of my facial pain and my anxiety reaction.

Temporomandibular Disorder Joint Dysfunction (TMJ or TMD)

Of all stress-related disorders, TMJ syndrome possibly may be the most misdiagnosed and most controversial. Even the name *TMJ* has recently (in 1983) been changed by the American Dental Association to *TMD*, standing for *temporomandibular disorder*.

Estimates of the number of people suffering from TMD have gone as high as seventy-five million Americans. Most specialists agree that women appear to make up the majority of sufferers.

Symptom Complex.

TMD pain is usually accompanied by ringing or buzzing in the ears, worn-down teeth, sinus problems, or pain in the areas of the jaw, face, and neck. In forming a diagnosis of TMD, most specialists will look for a clicking sound when the mouth is opened or closed, which is caused by the late slotting of a disk into position within the joint of the jaw.

Stress Related.

There is almost total agreement that chronic stress plays a definite and detrimental role in the development and continuation of TMD pain. Nighttime bruxism (teeth grinding) has been related directly to a person's inability to deal appropriately with stress. The tension is carried into his or her sleep cycle. This has been identified with TMD symptoms.

Have you ever seen anybody who has a tight-jaw personality? These people usually are anxious, overstressed, and easily angered. The dysfunctional emotions are translated into increased muscle tension, which keeps the muscles of the jaw in a constant state of muscle contraction. This possibly leads to a TMD condition. Most people can experience briefly what TMD is like by playing a reed instrument for a prolonged period of time, snorkeling, biting on a pencil, or cradling the telephone between shoulder and ear. These activities may irritate the temporomandibular joint and associated musculature, which can lead to pain.

Summary.

TMJ or TMD is a difficult pain condition to diagnose since it may duplicate the symptoms of dental problems, neck irritations, or head injuries. The causes of TMD include misalignment of the jaw due to: hereditary factors, accident, missing teeth, or stress. Additionally, the syndrome may be the result of teeth grinding (bruxism) or daily activities such as the way you use the telephone or continuous gum chewing.

Your Pain Relief Statement

We have established a definite connection between stress and TMD. The personalized pain relief formula, which includes the pain relief statement, will prove to be beneficial both in reducing the muscle tension behavior and overall discomfort and in short-circuiting your stress response.

This pain relief statement is to be inserted on day six into your personalized pain relief formula.

I am in control of my pain and stress.

Abdominal Pain

Abdominal pain may show itself through various conditions or diseases. Some of these are listed below:

Crohn's disease
Irritable bowel syndrome
Menstrual cramps
Ulcerative colitis
Ulcers

The list is not by any means complete. In many abdominal pain conditions, stress plays a significant role in the development and continuation of the pain. Ulcers and colitis are two of the more common conditions directly related to a person's inability to deal with stress appropriately.

(*Note:* If you have any sudden, incapacitating pain in your abdomen for more than thirty minutes or abdominal pain that awakens you at night, or if you experience any rectal bleeding, seek medical advice immediately.)

It's Stress Related.

If your physician has informed you that your abdominal pain, whether it be from ulcers, colitis, or irritable bowel syndrome, has its roots in your stress response, then you definitely need to use the Scottsdale Pain Relief Program for reducing the pain response and short-circuiting stress. Some of the conditions causing abdominal pain may disappear completely after appropriate use of the Scottsdale Pain Relief Program, especially if they are stress related.

The Stress Connection.

If you have been told that your pain is related directly to stress or that stress is increasing your pain, then you need to follow several steps to reduce and, in many cases, extinguish your pain.

Evaluate which stresses in your present environment may be reduced.

Complete the Scottsdale Pain Relief Program and utilize the Lifetime Maintenance Program.

Check with your physician about possible changes in your diet.

Become involved in an appropriate activity/exercise program that will serve as an excellent means for preventing buildup and releasing stressful reactions.

Your Pain Relief Statement

The pain relief statement should be inserted on day six. Do not forget to include the emotional part of the statement.

I am in control of my abdominal pain and emotions. (You may state specific emotions for further emphasis.)
Example: I am in control of my abdominal pain and anxiety.

Burns

Burns can be the most devastating and pain-producing conditions known. Some of the most difficult and heartwrenching times in my professional practice have involved working with burn pain patients, especially when pain medication had little or no effect on their suffering.

Patients suffering from burns have used the Scottsdale Pain Relief Program successfully as a means of coping with the constant, sometimes unbelievably severe pain following the initial burning and during the numerous medical procedures that are performed directly on the burns themselves. When you suffer from burns, it is always difficult to find a comfortable sleeping position. Burn patients have found that the Scottsdale Pain Relief Program has helped them control the devastation of their pain and allowed them to get more sleep and rest.

Emotional Benefits of the Program.

Besides the pain relief aspects of the Scottsdale Pain Relief Program, burn patients have used the personalized pain relief formula to help regain emotional control of the severe depression that often accompanies burn rehabilitation.

Your Pain Relief Statement

Your pain relief statement should be inserted on day six in your personalized pain relief formula.

I am in control of my pain and my body and my mind work together in the healing process.

Cancer Pain

In chapter four I will mention the work and study I have participated in with Dr. Carl Simonton. Some of my early ideas regarding pain control were stimulated by the teachings of Dr. Carl Simonton and Stephanie Mathews Simonton since these ideas they related to their work with cancer patients.

Numerous forms of cancer can be extremely painful, and over time traditional medications begin to lose their effectiveness. Patients with cancer who have used the Scottsdale Pain Relief Program not only use their pain control object for pain relief but also incorporate the concept of their white blood cells destroying the cancer and combine this with their mental imagery.

(*Note*: The Scottsdale Pain Relief Program and mental imagery for cancer should not be used as a substitute for appropriate medical diagnosis and treatment. They can serve as an excellent companion to therapy for anyone who experiences the devastation of cancer.)

Your Pain Relief Statement

The pain relief statement for cancer pain will be somewhat different from the other pain relief statements. The pain relief statement should be inserted into the personalized pain relief formula on day six.

I am in control of my ＿＿＿＿＿＿＿＿ [pain site,

pain condition, or cancer site] and my body attacks the cancer.

Sports Injuries

Ever since we have become a jogging, walking, bicycling, fitness-minded population, there has been a significant increase in sports injuries. Five years ago one would be hard-pressed to find a listing for a sports injury clinic in the physician's section of the phone book, but that has changed in direct proportion to the numbers of people who have taken on repetitive activities and exercises as part of their lifestyle.

Not Without Injuries.

The numbers and types of sports injuries appear to be increasing each year. Here is a list of just a few:

    Backache
    Exertion headaches
    Tension headaches
    Tendinitis
    Neck injuries
    Bone and joint injuries

You will notice immediately that many of the sports injuries are mentioned in other sections of this chapter. There is a significant degree of crossover.

You should never self-diagnose or self-treat a sports injury. Consult a qualified physician who specializes in them. If you find that even with appropriate medical treatment you still have the pain and discomfort, then you may want to use the Scottsdale Pain Relief Program.

Your Pain Relief Statement

Your pain relief statement for conditions related to sports injuries will be as follows:

I am in control of my _____ [pain site or pain condition] and my emotions are calm.

Additional Pain Segments with Pain Relief Statements

I have tried to present you with a variety of pain segments. Here are some additional pain conditions and situations along with pain statements.

Dental Pain.

I am in control of my _____ [pain site or condition].

Example: I am in control of my tooth pain.

Phantom Limb Pain.

I am in control of the pain in my _____ [pain site].

Example: I am in control of the pain in my arm.

Postsurgical Pain.

I am in control of my _____ [pain site] and my body and mind work together to help the healing process.

Example: I am in control of my shoulder pain and my mind and body work together to help the healing process.

Raynaud's Disease.

I am in control of my _____ [pain site] pain and my _____ [affected areas] are warm.

Example: I am in control of my hand pain and my fingers are warm.

If you are experiencing any pain that has not been discussed, and you have been evaluated by a physician, then follow these instructions.

Using the standard pain relief statement, insert your pain site or pain condition along with one of the following emotional control inserts:

Anxiety	Fear
Anger	Frustration
Depression	Self-confidence
Emotions	Self-worth
	Stress

Here is the pain relief statement to complete:

I am in control of my _____ [pain site or condition] and my _____ [emotional control insert].

Example: I am in control of my back pain and my depression.

When You Should See a Doctor Regarding Your Pain

You should call a doctor when:

The pain is new and you have never experienced it before.

There appears to be no explanation why the pain started.

Your usual pain has worsened progressively and continues to increase in intensity.

You are having a fever with the pain.

You cannot urinate.

You have bowel dysfunction.

The pain appears to be out of proportion to the injury or reason for discomfort.

Selecting an Appropriate Doctor.

We do it numerous times during our lives, but usually on the basis of family tradition or friends' recommendations. I'm talking about the selection of a doctor to evaluate or treat your pain condition.

I always tell my patients that the process of selecting a physician should be approached from a consumer's standpoint. Recommendations of friends or family should be an important part of the overall selection process, but you need to consider the physician's training, treatment philosophy, and willingness to be an active member of your treatment team. This team might be just yourself and the doctor, but it could include other specialists. There are three very important steps in the selection of a physician:

1. Checking his or her credentials, training, recommendations, and references from former patients

2. Determining his or her willingness to answer your questions

3. Listening: Does the doctor hear what you are saying?

Always remember that you are a consumer and there is absolutely nothing wrong with interviewing a prospective doctor who might play an important role in your medical care.

Chapter Four

The Scottsdale Pain
Relief Program

The Basics.

At last, here you are.

The tantalizing concept of controlling your pain—the main reason you are reading this book—is now within reach and yours for the taking. Like anything else that is achieved in life, there is hard work needed to develop the skills by which you, like so many others, will be able to gain control over your pain.

The basic program covers seven consecutive days and must be completed in the proper order. Following the end of the basic program, you will be directed to segments designed for your specific pain problem. These segments will provide you with more methods and suggestions for relief of your pain.

On day eight, you will begin the Lifetime Maintenance Program.

I have attempted to make all directions and instructions simple, straightforward, and easy to apply. There is no need for elaborate, expensive equipment or devices. The Scottsdale Pain Relief Program is not like that Christmas bicycle you struggled to assemble on December 24 with the instructions reading ''Simple Assembly—Only Screwdriver Needed.'' After numerous skinned knuckles, curses under your breath, and confusion over those ''simple'' instructions and diagrams, you neared the end of your task only to find the most vital part *missing*.

I will guarantee you that nothing is missing from the Scottsdale Pain Relief Program—since the single most important ingredient is *YOU*!

Using the Scottsdale Pain Relief Program.

To help you better understand and more fully use the Scottsdale Pain Relief Program, I have included the most common and frequently asked questions along with my answers.

Question: ''Will the Scottsdale Pain Relief Program take away all my pain?''

Answer: The program is designed to teach you how to control pain. The program in itself cannot reduce any pain but is simply a vehicle to be used by you for pain reduction and control.

Question: ''What if I don't have any built-in painkillers?''

Answer: Everyone has natural painkillers within their

body. These painkillers are called *endorphins* (for *endogenous morphinelike substances*) and are produced by the brain.

Question: "Can I start the program and then finish it at another time?"

Answer: No. The program should not be started unless you are committed to completing the full seven days without interruption.

Question: "How much time a day will I have to spend during the seven-day program?"

Answer: Usually everyone's time varies, but the minimum amount of time for successful completion of the program appears to be approximately sixty minutes per day.

Question: "Do I practice the program once a day?"

Answer: The more you practice, the greater the effectiveness of the pain relief formula. There will be a morning session and an evening session with daily practice. After you have developed your custom formula, it should only take you less than a minute to use the formula. You should practice as many times a day as possible, making pain relief a habit.

Question: "Will I have to practice for the rest of my life?"

Answer: Yes, but once your pain relief formula becomes a habit, you may only have to devote several minutes a day to it.

Question: "Are there any harmful side effects to the program?"

Answer: No. If you have obtained approval from your doctor regarding any physical restrictions, then there are no detrimental side effects from the Scottsdale Pain Relief Program.

Question: "Can the program be used with any type of pain?"

Answer: The Scottsdale Pain Relief Program has been designed to be capable of providing pain relief for any type of pain condition. Of course, you should have any pain condition diagnosed by a physician first to insure that the condition is not life threatening!

The Body/Mind Connection

The Body's Built-In Painkillers.

The nineteenth century provided us with the first glimpse of man's attempt to identify the body's built-in ability to conquer pain. The physicist James Clark Maxwell dabbled in many diverse areas, one of them being the athlete's endurance of pain. He was intrigued by the seemingly endless stories of top athletes performing to and beyond points of pain. Why could they keep going even when the very fibers of their exhausted bodies were trying to scream out in pain? What mechanism within them was activated to block this pain and allow them to continue?

The Brain Connection

The body is a tremendously complicated electrochemical system that is controlled significantly by your emotions, your outlook on life, and your ability to counteract the effects of stress, tension, anxiety, depression, and pain.

It is quite amazing to realize that the brain contains over one hundred billion nerve cells and even though almost none of these actually touch each other, they carry messages back and forth across gaps known as synapses. The degree to which messages are transported between nerve cells in the brain can be linked to neurotransmitters, which either slow down, block, or allow the messages to pass from one cell to another. Pain is one of these messages. It can be stopped or reduced by altering the brain's ability to pass a pain impulse from one cell to the next. Since the mid-1970s and the discovery of endorphins (the body's naturally produced painkillers), we have understood better some of the functioning that occurs with pain and the decrease of pain when these internal chemicals are produced. The simplest explanation of why endorphins work is that by slowing down the transmission of data (pain information), endorphins actually facilitate a decrease or block in our perception of pain.

The Automatic Response.

Although we can be certain the automatic response occurred before written history, we only have to go back through the course of recorded human existence to find examples of an inborn response for short-circuiting pain in survival situations.

Here are two modern-day examples of the automatic response.

CASE ONE.   The late-model sedan careened out of control on the icy highway, slewing from side to side until crashing broadside into a utility pole. Mrs. Cramer was thrown from the wreck and lay dazed on the gravel shoulder of the road. As consciousness gradually returned to her cloudy thoughts, she heard her eight-year-old daughter's screams coming from the shattered car. Somewhat unsteady at first, she stood up and ran toward the car as the first flames burst from underneath the engine compartment. She could see her daughter screaming and staring at her out the window on the driver's side. She reached the car and pulled open the door, lifting out her daughter in one swift motion. She ran as fast as she could and fell exhausted by the side of the road as the car erupted in flames, sending waves of blistering heat into the freezing night.

When the ambulance attendants checked the mother, they found that she had what appeared to be a severe fracture of her right forearm and a severely swollen ankle. She reported having felt no pain when she pulled her daughter from the car and raced to safety. Somehow her mind had produced painkillers that allowed her to save her daughter's life. She did not experience the excruciating pain of her injuries until safely in the ambulance.

CASE TWO.   It was third down and the home team needed eight yards in a game marked by mud, rain, and thudding impacts which could be heard all the way to the press box. Tom had played the whole game at defensive tackle. Through his exhaustion, he realized that if their defense could prevent the other team from gaining a first down, then his team could protect their slim lead and win the game. He focused his mind away from everything else and on the man in front of him. He prepared to summon every last ounce of strength for the charge into his opponent, which would lead him into the backfield and the opposing quarterback. All fatigue and exhaustion were pushed aside, and the mental picture of him pulling the quarterback into his grasp flashed through his mind. As if in a trance, his body exploded forward at the snap of the football, stepping left, moving right, and shouldering the blocker out of his way. Time seemed to elongate as he raced into the opponent's backfield with his only thought to reach the quarterback before he could throw the football. As the quarterback's arm pulled back, Tom lunged forward, driving his arms and shoulders into the quarterback's side and causing the ball to burst from his hand.

Tom ran to the sidelines with the cheers of the crowd ringing in his ears. He sat on the bench, took off his helmet, and reached for a squeeze bottle of water. The gun sounded.

They had won. Tom now allowed himself to feel an overwhelming sense of fatigue and exhaustion. It was not until he was removing his shoulder pads in the locker room that Tom found that two of the fingers on his left hand had been broken sometime during the game and only now throbbed as if they were on fire.

CASE THREE.   Kate had been playing outside with several other seven-year-olds from the neighborhood. She knew that her mother didn't want her to stand on her brother's skateboard, but she tried anyway. On the smooth driveway surface the skateboard shot out from under her, and she fell backward, scraping her elbow along the rough surface. There was sudden shock and pain, which increased as she looked at her arm and saw a beginning droplet of blood forming within the abrasion. Tears swelled in her eyes as she ran to the house calling for her mother. In the bathroom her mother washed the wound, put antiseptic on it, and applied a bandage. The scrape now hurt worse than when she had first injured the arm. The stinging and burning wouldn't go away, and Kate continued to sob. Her mother sat Kate on the couch and turned on the television. Through her sobs and pain, Kate heard familiar voices, and looking up she saw a Chip 'n' Dale cartoon. Within thirty seconds, Kate no longer felt the pain in her arm but was totally preoccupied with her favorite cartoon characters.

In each of these cases a mechanism within the body and controlled by the brain blocked the individual's pain. The length of time and the circumstances differed, but the basic fact remained the same: Each of us has the capability of blocking, reducing, and controlling pain. This is possibly a survival response passed on from our caveman ancestors and nearly lost from thousands of years of disuse.

Threshold versus Tolerance.

The point at which anyone becomes aware of pain is called the pain threshold or recognition level. This is the body's method of warning us of some malfunction or injury within our systems. The recognition level may vary from person to person. One individual might feel a paper cut on the finger as a minor discomfort, while another with a lower pain threshold experiences the injury as a more significant pain. The difference in each individual's perception of pain is known as the pain tolerance, which indicates how much pain someone can tolerate. We all know people who can withstand greater or lesser degrees of pain than we can.

One major objective of the Scottsdale Pain Relief Program is to increase your pain tolerance through production of the body's built-in painkillers. An advantage to this system lies in the fact that although someone's tolerance for pain might be increased, the pain threshold remains constant and therefore the body's warning signal will continue to effectively alert you to malfunctions or injuries.

If the body's built-in pain system were to cancel out automatically any pain within the body, then your safety would be in jeopardy. The only time the body appears to block out pain totally is during extreme trauma, in life-threatening situations, and only for a short amount of time.

Pain is very much like the horn on a car: It warns of impending problems and helps you avoid accidents. If the horn becomes stuck, then it no longer serves its warning purpose but becomes an irritant. The same applies to pain. When it continues on after the initial warning and results in chronic discomfort, then it becomes like a stuck horn.

It's in the Blood.

What better system is there within the body to transport the body's built-in painkillers? The blood travels to virtually every area of the body, from the tip of your tiniest toe to the top of your head. This miraculous transport system has been found to be the main carrier of the body's naturally produced opioids. Beta-endorphin was reported discovered in the circulation as early as 1977. The source of this opioid is believed to be the anterior and intermediate lobes of the pituitary gland. It is carried in the blood via the plasma. Enkephalin, also a circulating opioid, finds its source in the adrenal medulla of the brain.

From the beginning of my work with pain, I was aware of a phenomenon that occasionally took place in doctors' offices and hospitals. A patient, experiencing significant pain from a surgical procedure, was administered a shot of Demerol every four hours. After several days of injections, the doctor decided to stop them in favor of a weaker medication. The patient continued to complain of pain, and so the doctor decided to conduct an experiment. When the next shot was ordered, the doctor had the nurse administer a syringe of saline water instead of the Demerol. The nurse proclaimed to the patient that the shot would take effect in just a few minutes. Sure enough, upon the nurse's return, the patient commented on the wonderful pain-relieving qualities of the injection. In many cases the patient would then fall asleep, relaxed and in significantly less discomfort.

The use of saline injections, sugar pills, and other substitution devices has been known for many years to create an effect known as the placebo response. The patients think they have received something to reduce the pain, and their belief systems transmit that message to the brain, which in turn responds by producing the body's built-in painkillers. The patients mistakenly think the relief is due to the medication.

When Are the Opioids Produced?

Stress

Under severe stress, both physical and emotional, the body will automatically produce the opioid peptides (painkillers) and dump them into circulation, thus producing painkilling effects. Rarely does a day go by that we don't read in a newspaper of some traumatic incident such as the mother, critically injured in a car accident, who walks four miles to summon help for her unconscious child. The article goes on to state that the mother felt little pain, only numbness, as she struggled to save her daughter. We often hear a sports story like that of the professional football player who broke two fingers in the championship game but didn't notice the pain until the final gun sounded and he was sitting in the locker room, staring at his throbbing fingers.

Physical Exertion

Runner's High is a term that Wide World of Sports has popularized through their coverage of long-distance running events ranging from the Boston Marathon to the Iron Man Triathlon in Hawaii. Commentators, many of whom are former top athletes, will note during the middle and later stages of a race that the runners are experiencing a second wind or a runner's high. What does this phenomenon create for the runner? Many report a feeling of well-being, a sense of floating, and an ability to go beyond physical limitations. How does this mechanism occur? Study upon study has shown that under continued physical exertion the brain sends signals to opioid-producing stations within the body and there is a dramatic increase in blood plasma levels of beta-endorphin. Additionally, other circulating hormones and chemicals are produced that have been linked directly to reducing depression and anxiety.

Many of the world's top athletes actually train the body to the peak of conditioning. Besides gaining muscular strength and cardiovascular endurance, they are also training the body to produce its own built-in painkillers and emotion stabilizers on demand.

Acupuncture

Known for thousands of years throughout the Far East and China as a procedure for the elimination of pain, acupuncture is now gaining wider acceptance in the Western world. What mechanism within the body is activated through the skillful use of the acupuncture needle? Scientists seeking an answer to this question have found that plasma levels of opioids appear to increase with certain types of acupuncture. Medical researchers in China and other Eastern countries have written and talked of the body's ability to suppress pain. To them the notion is not new, but rather it is an accepted fact of life.

Their culture has always looked to mechanisms within the body to heal, to increase the body's tolerance to pain, or actually to diminish pain. Our culture has developed around the notion that the body is healed by medication, surgery, radiation—essentially everything outside of the body.

Sexual Activity

The feelings of ecstasy and pleasure experienced during intense sexual activity may be more than a product of one's fantasy, since the level of the body's built-in painkillers (beta-endorphins) increases dramatically with sexual behavior. This ability of the body is not limited just to one specific age group.

And All the Others

Hypnosis, self-hypnosis, trances, TM, food deprivation, pregnancy, isolation, hibernation, suggestion, and the placebo effect have all been shown to increase the body's tolerance to pain.

Your Built-In Painkillers

The Scottsdale Pain Relief Program will teach you how to develop the ability to activate your own built-in painkillers to decrease your specific pain. Once you have completed the seven-day program, then all of the skills needed to customize the formulas for your specific pain will be at your disposal.

Pain Control Imagery

The use of mental imagery as a technique for facilitating the combined efforts between mind and body has been well documented for years. Between 1975 and 1976, I had the opportunity to be in the first group of professionals training in a special program under the guidance of Carl Simonton, M.D. in Fort Worth, Texas. Dr. Simonton is an oncologist who, after years of using the traditional methods including radiation and chemotherapy to treat his cancer patients, became concerned that there was no alternative that involved the individual's own ability to fight cancer. He noted that some people would have "miraculous" remissions from what were considered fatal tumors, and he began to study the differences that might exist between these people and people with similar cancers who succumbed. His research led him back to the late 1800s when physicians had already begun to explore the relationship between the mind and the body and how an individual's thought process could affect his or her physical health. Once Dr. Simonton had established the link between the mind and body, he set about with coworkers to develop a program that could teach terminally ill cancer patients how to activate their immune system to destroy cancer cells. This involved the teaching of deep relaxation techniques combined with specialized mental imagery. Some patients imagined their white blood cells as Pac Man–like creatures traveling through the body to the site of the tumor and gobbling up the cancerous cells. Dr. Simonton's research indicated that patients who were capable of developing this type of mental imagery had a higher rate of remission than patients with similar conditions who were being treated through traditional means.

When I studied in Fort Worth, Texas, with Dr. Simonton, I had just established a pain center in Scottsdale, Arizona. I was treating cancer patients for their pain, but I felt that more could be accomplished. Unfortunately, the techniques used by Dr. Simonton at that time and further developed since lay somewhat dormant in my mind and in dusty notes in my office until about three years ago. Then a patient told me that during a deep relaxation session, she would imagine a big sponge traveling inside her body to the site of the pain. The pain was a green liquid that the sponge could soak up. The pain would decrease, and she would feel better. After she made these remarks, I went back to my notes and spent a considerable amount of time in the library researching the latest documents regarding the use of imagery. I concluded that this could be the missing link needed to help the pain sufferer activate, on a consistent basis, the body's built-in painkillers, the endorphins.

It took me almost a year to develop the specific formulas for teaching someone how to activate the body's built-in painkillers through the use of mental imagery. I will provide you with examples from some of my patients of how they applied their particular type of mental imagery to a specific pain problem. Of course, your mental imagery will be designed by you, for you. Because it will be customized to your circumstances, you will gain the greatest benefit.

Finally: The Formulas

By combining the use of autogenic therapy and mental imagery, I was able to complete the pain relief formulas. With the help of hundreds of patients, the program I am about to present to you represents the summation of research and trial and error, a product that has been proven to provide not only temporary pain reduction but also a plan to regain the ability to enjoy life through a Lifetime Maintenance Program.

Starting the Program.

Starting the Scottsdale Pain Relief Program is not merely a matter of reading the book and saying, "Well, I guess I'll start tomorrow." Preprogram preparation will be one of your keys to success.

Most people have found the best starting day to be a Saturday. This allows them Saturday and Sunday for adjustment to the routine. The following Saturday, you will begin the Lifetime Maintenance Program. The final choice as to starting day will be up to you, but allow at least a full day prior to day one for completion of the program setup.

All of the instructions in the preprogram should be followed carefully and completely. Completing the preprogram will take approximately two hours of uninterrupted time.

The Old Do's and Don't's.

Do follow the programs exactly from day to day

Do take your time

Do read through the entire program before beginning

Do practice the exercises and activities exactly as they are presented

Do involve your spouse or significant other if you desire

Do make sure you congratulate yourself for successes

Do discuss any physical changes that may occur with your physician

Don't skip any of the days

Don't get ahead of yourself

Don't expect too much, too soon

Don't expect the pain to disappear totally after seven days

Don't intermix any other techniques with this program

Don't plan any trips, vacations, or other significant activities during the seven-day program

Don't become frustrated

Don't change your practice times from day to day

Don't use this program as a substitute for proper medical care

What You Will Need.

Here's your list of items you will need prior to beginning the program. These should be available to you during the preprogram.

Two pencils

Colored markers or crayons

An 8" × 10" notebook or at least fifteen sheets of notebook-type, lined paper

Ten 5" × 7" index cards

One roll of cellophane tape

Optional: *A portable cassette tape recorder and two blank cassettes*

All of these items should be placed in one location along with your book.

A Place to Practice.

You will need to practice the morning and evening segments of your program at the same location, which should be a room that will provide you with a quiet, undisturbed environment. The room you select should have either a bed or lounge chair for your use. During practice sessions, any telephones in the room should be unplugged.

Insuring a quiet, undisturbed environment for your morning and evening segments is absolutely essential. If there are family members in your house, you will need to have a meeting with them prior to starting your program. By now, your spouse should be aware of the Scottsdale Pain Relief Program and you both should have taken time to review chapters one through four. This will have given you specific ideas for how to tell your family about the program and how to request their cooperation in an assertive manner. If you have prepared your family members properly, then their cooperation will help you to be successful. You don't have time in your program to be interrupted constantly with requests that could wait until after you have finished your practice.

Day by Day.

Day one of the Scottsdale Pain Relief Program will establish the routine that will be followed on days two through seven. Each daily program has been divided into three segments.

The Morning Program

This segment will take approximately twenty minutes for completion. It is to be performed while you are still in bed, at the same time each morning. The night before, you will review the next day's program and plan the coming day. The morning segment will consist of the pain control imagery and specific assignments that are to be completed during the day whether you are at home or at work.

The Day Program

Special practice assignments will be given during the morning segment that *must* be completed during the day (prior to 6:00 P.M.). These special practice assignments are to be performed once hourly for the first four days and twice hourly during days five through seven. Each practice segment will take no longer than twenty seconds for completion and during an average nine-hour day will require no more than six minutes of your time. The day program is designed not to interfere with any of your normal activities. Each of the seven day programs will differ slightly in content and direction, although the focus remains constant toward the development of a pain self-regulating system through repetition and constant reinforcement.

The Evening Program

The evening program will be performed just prior to your going to bed but should be at the same time each evening. This segment will take twenty minutes and will serve as a summary of the morning and day segments. Each evening program will be completed by a review of the next day's activities.

Pain Control Imagery

Putting It Together.

We've waited long enough. The time has now arrived for you to take the first step toward successful completion of the Scottsdale Pain Relief Program. Before beginning the seven-day program, you will need to develop some basics for your pain imagery.

Here is an outline of what I'm going to ask you to do and why.

1. *Pain Diagram.*

   The pain diagram will help you define more accurately the exact areas of your pain. The diagram will be used in your mental imagery as a targeting device. The diagram and pain areas will be used to provide target areas for your endorphins.

2. *Pain Color.*

   The pain color will be used to represent your discomfort. The most popular colors to describe pain appear to be red, black, and dark blue (or purple). You will learn how to develop your own color, which from this point on will represent pain.

3. *Pain Object(s).*

   Selecting your pain object or objects is an extremely important aspect of your total pain control imagery program and the development of your personalized pain relief formula. When you combine your pain object with the pain color, you will have your personalized representation of what pain would look like in your body. Be as graphic and detailed as possible. Once you have combined the pain object and the pain color, you will have the pain target for your built-in pain-killers (endorphins).

4. *Pain Control Color.*

The pain control color should be powerful. It is your representation of what color the endorphins are within your body. Some choices for the pain control color have been yellow, light blue, orange, and green.

5. *Pain Control Object(s).*

The pain control object or objects will also be part of your personalized representation of the body's built-in painkiller system. The pain object will be attacked by your pain control object. Make sure your pain control object is your own creation; don't rush or take someone else's suggestion. Take all the time you need and make sure that your pain control is a product of your own imagination and thought process.

(*Note:* If you have any difficulty imagining the color of either the pain object or the pain control object, don't become discouraged or try to force the imagery. If you are not successful on your first attempt, take a short break and then come back to try again. Mental imagery is a technique that all of us used as children, but unfortunately much of this ability was put to the wayside as we grew older. You never lost the ability, but it may take some effort and patience on your part, so don't be discouraged.)

Pain Diagram.

Using the figures provided in this book, you may mark your areas of pain by shading in pencil or tracing the diagram onto another piece of paper to complete your pain diagram. Do not throw this away for we are going to refer to it during the program.

Take a look at your diagram and evaluate it. Is this the area or areas where you are experiencing the most pain? If the site of your pain changes, then pick the most frequent area. Ask yourself the question, "If someone else were to look at my drawing, would they be able to describe where my pain is?" If your answer is yes, then you have successfully completed your pain diagram.

Pain Imagery.

For this exercise you may follow the same direction as the pain diagram either using the book or paper. Please do this alone, without the help of others, since the pain imagery has to be developed by you—to be used by you—to be effective for you.

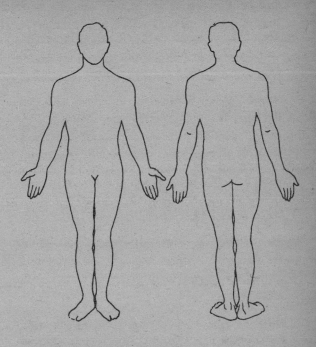

Pain Color

For all you budding artists, we are now going to pick a color to represent your pain. This exercise will take approximately five minutes. Follow the directions carefully.

1. Find a quiet place where you will not be disturbed for at least five minutes.

2. Lie down or sit in a comfortable chair, whichever is more convenient.

3. Take a deep breath in through your mouth and let it out slowly through your nose, closing your eyes as you exhale.

4. Breathe in and out nice and easy five times, taking in your breath through your mouth and exhaling through your nose. Count silently to yourself as you exhale each breath.

7. Now use your imagination and picture in your mind that you are standing in front of a blackboard with a piece of chalk in your hand.

6. Once the image of yourself standing in front of the blackboard is firm, take the chalk and write on your imaginary blackboard the word *pain* in large letters.

7. When you have completed the word, write the name of the first color that comes to mind below the word *pain*.

8. Now imagine yourself away from the blackboard, and in front of you on a table there is a large sheet of white paper.

9. Picture yourself writing on this large sheet of paper the word *pain* in the color you selected on the blackboard.

10. Picture the word *pain* in the color you selected clearly in your mind.

11. Open your eyes, and you now have your pain color.

You are now through the first exercise. If your family has been quiet and has not disturbed you, please don't forget to thank them. If they ask what you have been doing, share your exercise with them. By keeping them informed of the different exercises you do in the program and of your progress, you will allow them to become a positive factor in your Scottsdale Pain Relief Program rather than disinterested or confused observers.

The color you have selected to represent pain will now be used in all of your pain relief formulas to represent your particular pain. Once you pick the color, stick with it. Don't change once you start the program.

Pain Object(s).

To select your pain objects, you don't need to go through the same procedure that you did for your pain color. The pain objects will be used at the site of your pain and will be *your* pain objects. These objects are developed as part of your imagination, and they should be a visual imagery representation of what your pain means to you. To give you a few ideas, I have included some pain objects that people have used:

Tiny creatures with big claws and sharp teeth

Spiders

Crabs with big claws

Groups of X's

Clusters of dots

Worms with teeth

Fungi

Because the pain object should be the visual representation of your pain, if your pain is pinching, your objects may have claws. If your pain is stabbing, your objects may have spears or sharp claws.

Take a few minutes to think about your pain, referring to the information sheet where you described how your pain felt, and try to apply the characteristics to the pain objects you have selected.

Now take a sheet of paper and on it draw your pain objects. (*Note:* Use a pencil first to draw your pain objects and make any changes until they look like *your* pain. You will not be graded on your artistic ability. You should never have anyone else draw your pain objects since this has to be the representation you will use in the pain imagery.)

Pain Controllers

Pain Control Color.

To develop your pain controllers, you will need to make a return visit to that quiet place where you selected your pain color. Let anyone around you know that you will be busy for approximately five minutes and not to interrupt you. Use the following procedures:

1. Find as comfortable a position as possible, whether lying down or sitting.

2. Take a deep breath in through your mouth and let it out slowly through your nose, allowing your body to settle as much as possible.

3. Take five deep breaths, inhaling through your mouth and exhaling through your nose. As you exhale through your nose, silently count to yourself for each deep breath.

4. Try to clear your mind of any thought you might have as if you were painting over a window with white paint.

5. Now picture the most pleasant scene you possibly can, whether it be at the park, beach, countryside, or mountains. Fill in the scene with relaxing sights and sounds. This scene may represent a place where you have been before that you found to be very relaxing and enjoyable.

6. Place this scene firmly in your mind. Let your mind and body enjoy the serenity of the surroundings.

7. Now silently ask yourself what your favorite color is.

8. Picture this color in your mind. Notice how you get the same feeling as you do in your favorite scene. Open your eyes and sit up slowly, taking time to stretch your arms and legs gently.

Your favorite color is now your pain control color. This will be the color of the pain control objects you use in your pain relief formulas.

Pain Control Object(s).

If you have been following along carefully, you will know what we are going to do next. It's time to decide on the characteristic of your pain control objects. The pain control objects will be in your pain control color.

To help you, I have included a list of some pain control objects that have been selected and developed by people who have successfully used the Scottsdale Pain Relief Program. Remember, the objects have to be of your choice and should not be drawn or suggested to you by anyone else. The examples are only to serve as stimulus for your own imagination.

Tiny Pac Men (Women) that gobble up the pain objects

Cats that eat the pain objects

Tiny painters that paint over the pain objects with pain control colors

Sponges that absorb the pain control objects

Go now to the sheet of paper on which you drew your pain objects. Take a pencil and draw your pain control objects. Remember the standard practice in this book: No one's art is ever graded.

Congratulations. You now have your pain color, pain objects, pain control color, and pain control objects.

Pacing Yourself.

Slow and easy wins the race.

Haste makes waste.

These are statements familiar to all of us that are important in daily life. For someone experiencing a chronic pain condition, taking the time to plan ahead and pace yourself has an extra degree of importance. Whether you are a high-powered executive or a laid-back teacher, you will need to learn the basics of appropriate pacing.

The Pacing Commandments.

Read over the Pacing Commandments and think about how you might apply them to your specific work, recreational, or home situation. If you find yourself thinking, "Well, I'm sure that's very nice, but they really don't apply to me and I don't see any need to use them," then think about whether or not you would like the following statement to apply to you:

The use of appropriate pacing techniques will help to prevent reinjury or exacerbation of existing pain conditions and will allow for the maximum benefit of the Scottsdale Pain Relief Program.

Need I say more? Here are the commandments:

Never ride in a car for more than from forty-five to

sixty minutes without stopping for a five-minute break to stretch and use your pain relief formulas.

Never sit in one position for longer than from thirty to forty-five minutes without using your pain relief formulas.

Break difficult tasks into smaller segments, especially if they involve repetitive bending, lifting, stooping, or twisting.

Be assertive: don't accept tasks or assignments that you know will lead to possible reinjury or exacerbation of your pain.

Always use the intermissions at movies, plays, or concerts to your best advantage—by using them.

Don't feel obligated to keep up with someone else; go at an appropriate speed for you.

Probably the most important commandment is not even listed as one but is simply this statement:

Always listen to what your body is trying to tell you and then act upon its advice.

Optional Activities

Throughout development and use of the Scottsdale Pain Relief Program, I have strived constantly for simplicity. Busywork in filling out numerous forms will only sidetrack you from your purpose, which is completion of the seven-day program and learning how to use the Lifetime Maintenance Program.

Some people who have used the Scottsdale Pain Relief Program find the use of a diary to rate and graph their pain helpful, and therefore I have included it as an *OPTIONAL* part of your seven-day program. Additionally, patients have commented that the use of audio cassette tapes (self-recorded) were helpful during the morning and evening practice sessions. I have included some instructions regarding the recording of your own tapes, but making audio recordings of the practice session is an *OPTIONAL* part of the seven-day program.

Music to Your Pain.

The saying that music soothes the savage beast holds a higher degree of validity than most people realize. For years I have had quiet, relaxing music playing in the background in my office while treating patients. After a few moments, they consciously do not notice the music, but the relaxing quality of the sounds seems to enhance all of their treatments for pain.

Most of us have had the experience of listening to comfortable music and feeling a heightened state of relaxation or calmness.

The brain, through your sense of hearing, will utilize appropriate music to further a state of well-being, which is generated through production of the body's internal chemicals, especially painkillers and emotion-stabilizing substances.

Selecting Your Music.

If you plan to use music as part of your seven-day program, and I strongly recommend it, take some time to determine what sort of music gives you the greatest feeling of peace, tranquility, calmness, and overall sense of well-being. Most of my patients have preferred instrumental music, often with flowing rhythms that duplicate the heartbeat of the human body while at rest.

Once you have selected the appropriate music for you, you will need to place a tape recorder or record player in your private practice area to use for morning and evening practice sessions. While you are practicing, play the music as background sound, with the volume low. Playing music while you are practicing also serves to block extraneous noises or sounds that may interfere with your concentration.

Making the Final Selection.

The best way to make your final selection of music is to gather together the tapes or records (they should be at least thirty minutes in length) and go to your private practice area, lie down or sit in a comfortable chair, and listen to each one of your selections. Listen to your inner voice and evaluate how you are feeling physically and emotionally while you are listening to the music. The selection process should be relatively easy. If you find several pieces of music (at least thirty minutes in length) that provide you with feelings of well-being, then you may select them all and alternate their playing during your seven-day program.

Optional Pain Relief Formula Practice Tapes

Throughout my years of working with pain patients, I have tried constantly to design more effective ways to help people practice independently. The seven-day Scottsdale Pain Relief Program was designed for independent use. Although the program may be completed without recording any audio cassettes, people have reported that making the tapes facilitates practice and that using the tapes is easy and convenient.

I want to provide for every contingency that might enhance your success with the pain relief formulas. Therefore I have developed for the program an option of making audio cassettes of each day's practice sessions.

You may record the pain relief formulas in your own voice or that of a friend. Small cassette tape recorders are found in nearly every household or may be borrowed from a friend or neighbor. Using the tape recorder as a reinforcement device becomes another step toward increasing the probability of success.

In my own treatment I record pain relief imagery sessions and give the tape to the patient for practice until the next appointment. When my patients use the tapes, there is a noticeable improvement, especially in terms of utilizing the formulas as accurately as possible.

If you decide to record the pain relief formulas, then I strongly recommend that all recording be completed prior to your beginning the seven-day program. You will need seven blank cassettes with approximately thirty minutes on each side. Number the tapes from day one to day seven.

Write on the tape the exact name of the pain relief formula.

(*Note:* Never listen to the audio cassettes while driving, operating machinery, or experiencing a hazardous situation.)

Tips on Making Your Own Tapes.

1. Carefully read over the complete script for each exercise before you record. The scripts are designed for direct reading into the tape recorder, so you should read them aloud several times before making the final recording.

2. Choose a spot and a time where you will have absolute quiet. Distracting noises such as a telephone ringing, a child yelling, or a dog barking will interfere with your concentration when you listen to the tapes for practice.

3. Take your time! Read the sentences in a relaxed voice. Try to develop a rhythm in your speech.

4. Be careful not to speak too close to the microphone, as this might garble your voice and result in static. Run through a test session to see how far away from the mike you should speak.

5. After you have completed a tape, listen to it and compare it with the script.

6. If the tape is satisfactory, then punch out the tiny plastic tab in the back of the cassette. When this is done, the tape cannot be recorded over by accident.

The tab on the right is for side one and the one on the left is for side two.

Pain Relief Reminders

"I just forgot."

"I was so busy, I forgot."

"I could remember if someone set an alarm for me or reminded me."

"I was so mad when I realized that two hours had gone by without practicing."

These are common statements made to me by people going through the seven-day program. As a natural consequence of human nature, we all can become distracted and preoccupied. Unfortunately, missing several of the daily practice sessions, especially toward the end of the seven-day program when they become more intense, can lead to a decrease in the program's potency. The pain relief reminders have been developed as one technique to help you be consistent and punctual in your daily practice.

Rubber bands around wrists, strings around fingers, notes in pockets and purses, and even writing on your hands have been techniques used by people to remind them of something that has to be done. Pain relief reminders are simply what their name implies. They are little tricks you may use as reminders for your daily practice. Each individual's lifestyle is different, and their home and work situations will demand different types of reminders. When you see one of *your* reminders, there will be an immediate recognition and stimulus provided to remind you of the practice sessions required for each day of the program. Don't think the reminders are for the seven-day program only, for I'm going to ask you to continue using them even into the Lifetime Maintenance Program.

Be innovative and creative in the development of your pain relief reminders. After you use one reminder for a while, don't hesitate to change to another. If you find a reminder not working so successfully as you would like, don't hesitate or delay in changing it.

The following list represents a sampling of reminders used successfully by people in the Scottsdale Pain Relief Program.

Colored adhesive dots that can be placed on objects like telephones, desks, refrigerators, watch dials, daily calendars, and clocks

Special markings made at the appropriate times in appointment books

Asking your secretary, spouse, or coworker to help remind you, especially during the first several days (but do not rely on other people totally for your reminders; the interpersonal reminder should be combined with at least one other type of pain relief reminder)

Rubber bands on wrists

Reminder cards placed on everyday objects like desks, calendars, and car seats

The Day Before.

You start the seven-day program tomorrow. All the information and facts that you will need for successful completion of the program have been presented to you in chapters one, two, and three. By coming this far, you have shown a definite commitment, so don't turn back now. You should already have reviewed day one and taken a brief look at days two through seven. You have allotted time for the morning and evening sessions, and you have selected a pain relief reminder to help with the hourly practice sessions during the day from 9:00 A.M. to 6:00 P.M.

Everything is at your fingertips. Now all that remains is for you to begin the program.

If you are feeling a slight bit of nervousness along with hopeful anticipation, these emotions are quite normal.

I wish you the best and smoothest of journeys as you embark upon your final expedition in search for pain relief. Your reward is now coming into sight.

I have said it before, and I'll probably say it again and again throughout the book, don't be afraid to go back and review, spending all the time you need to understand fully each one of the chapters.

What You Will Do Each Day.

Each day of the program you will be presented with specific tasks to complete and formulas to practice. Don't let the simplicity and ease of directions fool you—the program has been designed for maximum impact on your specific pain problem.

Each day you will be required to do the following:

Morning practice (twenty minutes)
Daily practice (twenty seconds or less every hour until 6:00 P.M.)
Evening practice (twenty minutes)

There is definitely a necessary time commitment for each day of the seven-day program. You have to decide for yourself whether a commitment of approximately sixty minutes total time per day for participation in a program that will teach you how to obtain relief from your pain is worth the time. Let me give you a little hint and, possibly, a slight nudge. Recent time management studies indicate that all of us, whether at work or at home, waste approximately two-and-a-half hours per day that could be used for productive endeavors. The bottom line is that even with participation in the Scottsdale Pain Relief Program, you will still have one-and-a-half hours per day to waste if you so desire. After giving you this information, and if you were sitting in front of me, I would now challenge you to tell me that you don't have time during your day to participate in a program that has the potential of changing the rest of your life.

Most people who have participated in the Scottsdale Pain Relief Program have little problem committing to twenty minutes in the morning and twenty minutes in the evening for practice, but they do experience some difficulty, at least in the beginning, remembering to practice the pain formulas on an hourly basis. The pain relief reminders will help you by insuring consistent practice during the day.

Preprogram Checklist.

Step by Step: At this point you are ready to begin the seven-day program. Please review the steps to make sure you have completed each one before starting day one.

1. Read chapters one through three.
2. Discuss program with family or significant others.
3. Develop pain color and object(s).
4. Develop pain control color and object(s).
5. Obtain all materials needed for the seven-day program as listed on Page 105.
6. Review day one.

If you have completed all of the steps, then it's time to begin controlling your pain.

Day One

Introduction.

Day one is about to start. Chapters one, two, and three gave you the basics, but now comes the true test of your commitment. Although I have suggested that you review the complete program prior to starting, don't get ahead of yourself. Take each day one at a time with occasional glances to the future.

Daily Review.

On each of the seven days, the daily review section will go back to highlight important aspects of the previous day's program. The review will be presented in a checklist format, and you will be asked to read each statement and answer either yes or no. If you should answer no to any question, go back to the prior day and reread that material or redo the assignment until you can answer yes to the statement. When you answer yes to all the statements, then continue to the day's pain relief formula.

Here is your first day's review. Answer yes or no to each statement.

1. Is the body capable of producing its own pain-killers?

2. Do I understand the connection between emotions and pain?

3. Have I set aside special times in the morning and evening for practice?

If you have answered yes to all the statements, go on to today's pain relief formula. If you have answered no to any statement, then go back to review that area until you can answer the statement with a yes.

Today's Pain Relief Formula.

The Pain Relief Scan

The Basics.

One of the best ways for you to begin short-circuiting the pain is with the pain relief scan, which combines a specialized breathing technique with a method for reducing muscle tension or bracing.

Think back to the last time you were frightened, angry, stressed, or in severe pain, and remember how you were breathing. Most of the time your breathing changes under stress or with pain. Breathing becomes rapid, with high-in-the-chest inhalation and exhalation patterns. This type of breathing sends a message to the brain, which interprets it as danger or the fight/flight response (the extreme anxiety response that is triggered when danger or overwhelming stress is perceived and activates processes such as increased respiration, increased heart rate, and decreased blood flow to the extremities). The way you short-circuit this response is to learn a method to control your breathing and send a message to the brain that you are relaxed and in control.

The second part of the formula is the scan. When you are in pain, the muscles of the body become tense and tight, reducing the body's ability to transport fuel (oxygen, nutrients, and essential chemicals) to the muscles and carry away the waste products of muscle contraction.

Relaxed breathing and muscles enhance the body's ability to produce and use effectively its built-in painkillers.

Goals.

The pain relief scan will accomplish the following:

It will stop the stress/pain breathing response.

It will reduce muscle tension.

It will reduce pain.

Instructions.

The pain relief scan will be used to start all of the pain relief formulas. Follow the instructions carefully, reading them over completely several times before you begin.

Close your eyes.

Inhale deeply through your nose.

Hold the breath for a silent count of six.

Exhale slowly through your mouth.

(Repeat five times.)

With your eyes still closed, start at the top of your head and imagine as if someone had just begun to pour pleasantly warm water on your hair and the warmth was beginning to gently glow down your body. Picture in your mind's eye (mental imagery) the warm liquid slowly moving down your body and relaxing all the muscles it passes over.

Stop at any muscles that seem tense or tight or where you are having any pain.

Don't rush; take your time.

Keep your breathing calm and regular.

(When you reach your feet, there will be a general sensation of heaviness in the body and you may feel some warmth in your arms and legs.)

Repeat the breathing part of the formula five more times, silently counting to six while you hold your breath and then exhaling slowly through your mouth.

Take one deep breath, letting it out in a regular manner. Open your eyes, gently stretch your arms and legs, and get up slowly.

(*Important Note:* Never stand up quickly or jump up following the practice of a formula—you could become faint or dizzy and fall!)

Today's Practice

Morning Session.

TIME = Twenty minutes

REPETITIONS = Twice

FORMAT: Perform the complete formula while lying down or sitting in a comfortable chair. Use your private practice setting.

Daily Sessions.

TIME   =   Twenty seconds

REPETITIONS   =   Once every hour from 9 A.M. until 6 P.M. Don't forget to use the Pain Relief Reminders.

FORMAT:

Take one pain relief breath.

Hold the breath for a silent count of four.

Exhale slowly through your mouth.

Mentally picture your body and see any area where there is tension, tightness, or pain.

In your mind's eye gently pour the warm water on the areas.

Feel the relaxation.

Take one regular deep breath and let it out slowly.

(*Note:* This formula may be practiced with eyes open or closed. Use it both ways since it will be important to be able to activate the formulas with your eyes open under certain circumstances where it would be inappropriate to close your eyes such as driving, in a meeting, at work.)

Evening Session.

Repeat the twenty-minute morning session, in its entirety, twice.

Day One in Review

You have now completed the first day of the seven-day program, and you should congratulate yourself. Don't rest on your laurels too long, though, for we have more work to do. Go back through the day's activities and see if there were any problem areas. If you had difficulty using your practice area for the morning and evening sessions, then plan for any needed changes now—don't wait until tomorrow. If you missed an hour during the daily practice, don't despair or become discouraged; do something about it. Plan ahead for tomorrow.

Remember to go back to any of the previous chapters for review if you have any questions.

Today you have learned:

The first pain relief formula

The pain relief scan

How to practice hourly during the daily practice sessions

Day Two

Introduction.

Today we are going to learn basic imagery. This will be the starting point for your personalized pain relief formula. Like any other technique in the Scottsdale Pain Relief Program, basic imagery will take practice, commitment, and your willingness to try something new.

Daily Review.

Your daily review for today will cover day one. Please answer yes or no to each of the following statements.

1. Will proper breathing short-circuit the emotional response to pain?

2. Am I able to visualize my pain areas?

3. Is my location for morning and evening practice sessions adequate?

4. Are my pain relief reminders working?

If you have answered yes to all of the statements, go on to today's pain relief formula. If you have answered no to any statements, then go back to review that area from day one until you can answer the statement with a yes.

Today's Pain Relief Formula.

Basic Imagery

The Basics.

This pain relief formula is designed specifically for you to use as the first step toward development of your personalized pain relief formula. Basic imagery must be accomplished prior to your use of the pain objects and pain control objects.

The use of mental imagery (basic imagery) will allow you to create scenes and situations through your imagination. If this is performed with enough clarity, your brain will activate an emotional and physical response that will be compatible with your imagery.

Mental imagery is not automatic and needs to be practiced and refined to reach its peak of effectiveness. Whenever you practice your imagery, strive for the clearest, most vibrant picture. Use colors and movement if possible. It may take practice before you will be able to use color in your imagery.

Goals.

Basic imagery will accomplish the following:

It will help you mentally to define your pain areas.

It will reduce muscle tension.

It will reduce pain.

Instructions.

Basic imagery will follow the pain relief scan. Follow the instructions carefully, reading them over completely several times before you begin.

Close your eyes.

Inhale deeply through your nose.

Hold the breath for a silent count of six.

Exhale slowly through your mouth.

(Repeat five times.)

Clear your mind of any extraneous thoughts.

Count silently to yourself from twenty to one, repeating each number as you exhale.

When you reach the number one, mentally picture in your mind the most comfortable, enjoyable, relaxing scene that you possibly can. This scene may be in the countryside, by a running stream, or on a sunny, deserted beach with the sounds of waves in the background.

Try to picture your scene as completely as possible.

(*Note:* As you mentally imagine your scene, don't be afraid to put yourself into that scene, sensing smells and sounds, as if you were actually there.)

See yourself in this scene.

Notice how relaxed and completely at peace you are.

Stay in this scene for as long as you would like but with increasing clarity imagine as though you were an artist filling in a beautiful painting.

Keep your breathing calm and regular.

Repeat the breathing part of the pain relief scan five times, silently counting to six while you hold your breath, and then exhaling slowly through your mouth.

Take one deep breath, letting it out in a regular manner. Open your eyes, gently stretch your arms and legs, and get up slowly.

Today's Practice

Morning Session.

TIME = Twenty minutes

REPETITIONS = Once

FORMAT: Perform the complete basic imagery.

Daily Sessions.

TIME = Twenty seconds

REPETITIONS = Once every hour from 9:00 A.M. to 6:00 P.M.

FORMAT:

> *Take one pain relief breath.*
>
> *Hold the breath for a silent count of four.*
>
> *Exhale slowly through your mouth and allow your shoulders and arms to relax and sag slightly.*
>
> *Using your basic imagery, place yourself in your favorite scene.*
>
> *Picture the scene as vividly as possible for ten seconds.*
>
> *Sense the calm and peaceful control.*
>
> *Take one regular deep breath and let it out slowly.*

(*Note:* As with day one's formula, I would like you to practice your basic imagery with your eyes open at least twenty-five percent of the time. I know this is difficult, and the first time you practice the basic imagery with your eyes open, you may only be able to develop a partial scene. This is all right. It will improve as you practice.)

Evening Session.

TIME = Twenty minutes

Repeat the morning session in its entirety, but this time try to picture your scene more quickly (without rushing too much) and spend more time placing yourself within the imagery. Be aware of what you are doing and try to sense the deep, controlled relaxation you should feel in that scene.

Day Two in Review

Day two has been demanding. Basic imagery requires you to use skills that you once had as a child and may have been forced to give up in the face of the sometimes harsh realities of life. You have not lost these skills. All of us have them within our reach, although it may take some effort to regain their use after many years.

If you would like to practice an additional twenty-minute segment after your evening session, please feel free to do so, but follow the exact procedure that you used during the day. At this point in the program do not attempt to change any of the formulas, for this may reduce their effectiveness and adversely affect your progress later in the program.

Today you have learned:

Basic imagery

How to combine the pain relief scan breathing technique with basic imagery

Day Three

Introduction.

As you enter day three of the program, you are starting to develop good practice habits and your body and mind are being trained to help you learn to control your pain.

Daily Review.

Although the daily review may seem rather simple and uncomplicated at times, never skip answering the statements.

Here is your third day's review. Answer yes or no to each statement.

1. Have I been able to develop my scene through mental imagery?

2. Is the breathing segment of the pain relief scan, which is used to begin each practice session, becoming more automatic?

3. Have I evaluated my pain relief reminders?

Today's Pain Relief Formula.

Pain Control Imagery

The Basics.

The time has arrived finally for you to use your pain control object(s). At this time go back and take a look at the section on your pain control object(s). Today we are going to take that pain control object and integrate it into your basic imagery. The integration of your pain control object into *your* favorite scene will present your first big challenge. You will be successful if you follow these simple guidelines:

> *Do not force yourself or become angry if you have difficulty with your imagery.*
>
> *If you become distracted, gently bring yourself back to your scene.*
>
> *Insure during your morning and evening session that you are not interrupted.*

By now you should have noticed that each formula builds upon the previous day's work, as we gradually but steadily move toward the development of your personalized pain relief formula, which will be developed fully on day five. Your progress will improve if you maintain your natural rhythm and listen to your inner pacing.

Goals.

The pain control imagery will accomplish the following:

> *It will improve your skills in mental visualization.*
>
> *It will begin the integration of your pain control object into your favorite scene.*
>
> *It will improve your ability in the twenty-second practice sessions.*

Instructions.

The pain control imagery will utilize a combination of your favorite scene and your pain control object. Review your pain control object before beginning this session.

Follow the instructions carefully, reading them over completely several times before you begin.

Close your eyes.

Inhale deeply through your nose.

Hold the breath for a silent count of six.

Exhale slowly through your mouth.

(Repeat five times.)

Use the second part of your pain relief scan and allow the sensation of warm water to flow from your head to your toes.

Clear your thoughts.

Using the basic imagery, develop your special scene, putting yourself into the scene as much as you possibly can.

Focus on yourself within the scene.

Visualize that your hand is opened, palm up.

Place your pain control object in the palm of your hand.

Notice that the palm of your hand and your arm feel comfortably warm and relaxed.

Sense how comfortable you feel holding the pain control object in the palm of your hand.

Visualize the pain control object in its pain control color.

Notice how the warmth increases when you picture the pain control object in its color.

Notice how the pain control object appears to radiate a pulsing, vibrant sensation.

Now visualize that the pain control object, in its color, is becoming absorbed into the skin of your hand.

As the pain control object is absorbed, notice that your hand feels warmer, just as if you were placing it near a warm light bulb.

When the pain control object has disappeared into the skin of the palm of your hand, take one deep breath, letting it out in a regular manner. Open your eyes, gently stretch your arms and legs, and get up slowly.

Today's Practice

Morning Session.

TIME = Twenty minutes

REPETITIONS = Once

Daily Sessions.

TIME   =   Twenty seconds

REPETITIONS   =   Once every hour from 9:00 A.M. to 6:00 P.M. You may practice more than once an hour if you desire.

FORMAT:

Take one pain relief breath.

Hold the breath for a silent count of four.

Exhale slowly through the mouth.

Use your visual imagery to picture your pain control object in the palm of your hand. You do not need to place yourself in your favorite scene, but instead look at your hand and visualize the pain control object, in its color, sitting in your palm.

Visualize the pain control object being absorbed into the palm of your hand.

Feel the increased warmth and relaxed sensation as the pain control object is absorbed into your hand.

Take one regular deep breath and let it out slowly.

Evening Session.

TIME   =   Twenty minutes

REPETITIONS   =   Once

Repeat the morning session in its entirety, concentrating on the absorption of the pain control object into the palm of your hand and always being aware of the pleasant sensation occurring as this process takes place. With increased practice, the warm, pleasant sensation you experience as the pain control object is absorbed into your hand will begin to spread up your arm and to other parts of your body.

Day Three in Review

For many this has been a difficult day. I am asking you to reach deep inside yourself and explore the limits of your mental imagery abilities although you are only three days into the Scottsdale Pain Relief Program. Before I developed the Scottsdale Pain Relief Program, I would have had to spend from one to two weeks just learning the basics and then up to four or five weeks training in an elementary type of pain control imagery. Times have changed, and I am sure you do not want to wait five weeks to get into your pain relief formula. Don't be discouraged. Keep practicing and moving forward!

Today you have learned:

Pain control imagery

The first step in learning your pain control imagery

The first step in using your pain control object

The use of mental imagery in a present-tense situation (the daily practice sessions)

Day Four

Introduction.

As we move into day four, there may be a slight frustration on your part, especially if you are pushing too hard. As I've said previously, sit back, take your time, don't rush, and pay close attention to your natural pacing. The feelings and sensations you experience following a good meal, an enjoyable movie, or a walk on a beautiful day will activate a calm inner pacing.

Today we are going to take your pain control object on a trip in your body. For the first time, you will meet up with your pain object(s).

The time has come for your pain control objects to earn their pay and go to work providing you with pain relief.

Daily Review.

The review of your first three days will be slightly more comprehensive. Answer yes or no to each statement.

1. Am I capable of visualizing my pain control objects?

2. Am I capable of visualizing my pain control object in (pain control) color?

3. Upon exhaling the first pain relief breath of any practice session, am I beginning to feel a greater sensation of overall body relaxation?

4. Has my practice schedule become automatic?

If you have answered yes to all the statements, go on to today's pain relief formula. If you have answered no to any statement, then go back to review or practice that area until you can answer the statement with a yes.

Today's Pain Relief Formula.

The Beginning Journey

The Basics.

The belief in your ability to activate your built-in painkillers should be something you never doubt. At times during the seven-day program you may question it, but never doubt the capability of your own body to control pain, as long as you are willing to provide the time and practice.

In today's formula, your pain control object will be going on a journey to one of the most exclusive destinations in the world: the inside of your body. In the course of its journey, it will come into contact with the pain object.

Goals.

Pain relief formula four—the beginning journey—will accomplish the following:

It will begin the built-in painkiller activation process.

It will allow your pain control object to move within your body.

It will develop the visualization of your pain object.

Instructions.

Today's formula will be your most challenging endeavor, and therefore I suggest you read it a minimum of three times before attempting the practice sessions.

Follow each of the instructions carefully and do not move any faster than your normal, relaxed rate of breathing (inner pacing).

Close your eyes.

Inhale deeply through your nose.

Hold the breath for a silent count of six.

Exhale slowly through your mouth.

(Repeat two times.)

Perform your pain relief scan, starting at the top of your head.

Place yourself in your favorite scene.

Visualize your pain control object, in its color, resting in the palm of your hand.

Visualize and sense the increasing warmth and vibrancy of the pain control object as it begins to dissolve into the palm of your hand.

Notice the warmth as the pain control object disappears.

With your visualization, see the color of your pain control object faintly as it moves up your arm and begins to spread throughout your body.

As your pain control object travels throughout your body, feel an increase of warmth, heaviness, and general well-being.

Now move away from the scene of yourself and picture the pain object, in its color.

Notice that when you visualize the pain object the feeling of well-being that you had previously begins to disappear.

Again, visualize yourself in a favorite scene.

Think where you are experiencing the most pain or discomfort at this moment.

Picture your pain object in that part of your body where you are having the most pain or discomfort.

Notice how the pain object's color shows through the skin where you are experiencing pain.

Notice how the pain increases slightly as you focus on the pain object.

Visualize your favorite scene and place yourself there.

Imagine your whole body and see the pain object at its location.

Now picture in your mind's eye your pain control object in the palm of your hand, warm and vibrant.

Visualize the pain control object dissolving into the

*palm of your hand and beginning to move on a jour-
ney throughout your body toward the pain object.*

*Feel a sensation of warmth, relaxation, and well-
being as the pain control object spreads and moves
towards the pain object.*

*Take one deep breath, letting it out in a regular man-
ner. Open your eyes, gently stretch your arms and
legs, and get up slowly.*

Today's Practice

Morning Session.

TIME   =   Twenty minutes

REPETITIONS   =   Once

(*Note:* If you want to spend additional time in your morning session, please do not restrict yourself to the twenty-
minute schedule.)

FORMAT: Perform the complete beginning journey formula.

Daily Sessions.

TIME   =   Twenty seconds

REPETITIONS   =   Once every hour from 9:00 A.M. to 6:00
P.M. I recommend practicing more than once per hour if

possible, but this does not have to be accomplished consistently.

FORMAT:

Take one pain relief breath through your nose.

Exhale slowly through your mouth.

Visualize your pain object(s) at the site of the pain you are experiencing.

(*Note:* If you are not experiencing pain at the time of your practice session, then visualize the pain object at the usual site of your pain.)

Picture in your mind's eye the pain control object dissolving quickly into the palm of your hand and spreading throughout your body.

Picture the pain control object at the site of your pain object.

Take one regular deep breath through your nose and exhale normally through your mouth.

Evening Session.

TIME   =   Twenty minutes

REPETITIONS   =   Once

Repeat the morning session in its entirety, but try to visualize the pain control object entering the body more quickly and spreading throughout the body at a faster rate.

At this point, the pain control object is still not to come into contact with the pain object.

Day Four in Review

You are now over halfway through your seven-day program. I know it has been demanding, but the rewards are yours for the rest of your life.

Tomorrow you will gain the final ingredient prior to the full development of your personalized pain relief formula. Once you have your personalized pain relief formula, you will find the hourly practice sessions to be more productive. Most people start practicing their personalized pain relief formulas more than once per hour.

Today you have learned:

The beginning journey

How to spread your pain control object throughout your body

The placement of your pain object at your pain site

Day Five

Introduction.

Today is a big day. You will be given the final ingredients for your personalized pain relief formula. At this point in the program, I would like you to go to chapter three and read the segment that relates to your specific pain. In each pain segment, there are suggestions relating to the customized aspect of your personalized pain relief formula.

Daily Review.

The daily review for today will be short and to the point. By this point in the program, you should be reviewing on a daily basis those items that are still somewhat unclear or trigger further questions. Most people would find it difficult to progress this far in the program without a good foundation of knowledge gained in the first three chapters and the first four days of the Scottsdale Pain Relief Program.

Here is your review for day five. Answer yes or no to each statement.

1. Does the pain relief object serve as an automatic activating device for the body's built-in painkillers (endorphins)?

2. Will the reduction in size and number of the pain objects be related directly to decreased pain and increased pain tolerance?

If you have answered yes to both these statements, go on to today's pain relief formula. If you have answered no to either statement, then go back to review that area until you can answer the statement with a yes.

Today's Pain Relief Formula.

Your Personalized Pain Relief Formula—Part One

The Basics.

Your personalized pain relief formula—part one is the initial step toward the finalization of a formula that has the capability of being activated fully, anywhere, anytime, and under any circumstances, in less than thirty seconds.

Although the previous four days of the program have been extremely important, I cannot overemphasize the need for you to become completely and totally absorbed in today's lesson along with days six and seven.

By now many of you have already begun to experience some pain relief along with beneficial emotional consequences such as less depression and anxiety and a more positive attitude toward yourself and your environment. Do not let your success lull you into complacency. The most difficult and demanding three days of the program are ahead of you, so take a deep breath, let it out slowly, and let's begin.

Goals.

Your personalized pain relief formula—part one will accomplish the following:

It will allow direct interaction between your pain control object and the pain object.

It will be the first of three parts to your finalized personalized pain relief formula.

It will allow continued pain reduction.

It will provide improved psychological and emotional functioning and coping.

Instructions.

Your personalized pain relief formula—part one will be shorter in overall length than yesterday's formula, but you will be required to practice it more times during your morning and evening sessions. The shorter formula and increased practice sessions begin a conditioning process designed to develop your capabilities for activating your personalized pain relief formula in the shortest period of time possible with the highest degree of effectiveness.

Follow the instructions carefully, reading them over *twice* before you begin.

Close your eyes.

Inhale deeply through your nose.

Exhale slowly through your mouth.

Using your mental imagery, visualize the pain control object, in its color, resting in the palm of your hand.

Picture through mental imagery the pain object in its color, at your pain site.

Take a deep breath in through your nose and slowly let it out through your mouth, and as you do so, visualize the pain control object dissolving into the palm of your hand.

Visualize the color of your pain control object moving to all parts of your body, initiating a warm, heavy, and peaceful feeling and sensation.

As if you were a movie camera zooming in for a close-up, mentally picture your pain object.

(*Note:* If you have more than one pain site, visualize the most severe pain site at this time.)

Visualize the pain control object beginning to interact (eat, dissolve, cover, attach) with the pain object.

Visualize the pain object becoming slowly smaller.

Take one deep breath, letting it out in a regular manner through your mouth. Open your eyes, gently stretch your arms and legs, and get up slowly.

(*Note:* If you are going to repeat the formula or continue with the visualization, do not take this final step. Perform it only at the conclusion of your session.)

Today's Practice

Morning Session.

TIME = Twenty minutes

REPETITIONS = Once, but the imagery should be continuous until the end of twenty minutes.

FORMAT: Perform your personalized pain relief formula—part one for a full twenty minutes. Some people will find the process of removing the pain object to be quite difficult and at the end of fifteen minutes may have only removed, destroyed, or dissolved a portion. This is perfectly all right because you may never totally or completely rid yourself of the pain object. Remember, our purpose is to reduce the pain object to a point where it is no longer adversely affecting your physical or emotional well-being.

In the morning session, when you reach the interaction point between the pain control object and the pain object, continue with that part of the visualization if you have additional time. Do not complete the entire exercise and then start again.

Daily Sessions.

TIME = Twenty seconds

REPETITIONS = Twice every hour (every thirty minutes) from 9:00 A.M. to 6:00 P.M. Practicing on a twice-hourly basis will be difficult; I fully understand this, but if we are going to make the kind of progress I am sure you want, then there has to be a commitment to twice-hourly practice. If you should feel the desire and have the time to practice more than twice an hour, please do so. Remember that even if you were to practice three times per hour, the total time used would only be *one minute*.

FORMAT:

Take one pain relief breath and exhale slowly through your mouth.

Mentally visualize your pain control object(s) attacking the pain object(s).

Take one regular deep breath and let it out slowly through your mouth.

Evening Sessions.

TIME = Twenty minutes

REPETITIONS = Once

Use the daily practice technique for initiating the visualization process. Then begin your visualization of the pain control object destroying the pain object. If you should become fatigued or notice that you are being distracted, switch visualization to your favorite scene, allow yourself to relax fully, and once you feel reenergized, then begin visualizing the pain control object destroying the pain object once again.

(*Note*: If you want to go longer than twenty minutes, I would recommend that you do not. Instead of going longer in the evening session, I would rather that you use the daily session technique and practice using a twenty-second time span.)

Day Five in Review

You have now completed part one of your personalized pain relief formula. Increased practice is going to be extremely important. I would rather you practice with twenty-second segments instead of long, intensive sessions. Your intentions at this point are twofold:

1. To activate the pain relief formula as quickly as possible

2. To develop the activation of the pain relief formula as an unconscious habit

Earlier in the day you read your pain segment in chapter three. Now I would like you to read tomorrow's program and learn how you will be applying the pain segment to your personalized pain relief formula—part two.

Today you have learned:

To begin the destruction of your pain object(s)

To initiate the beginnings of your personalized pain relief formula

To begin using the personalized pain relief formula on an unconscious-habit basis

Day Six

Introduction.

As you enter day six of the Scottsdale Pain Relief Program, you are one step away from your personalized pain relief formula in its final form. Today you will be shown how to incorporate the pain segment into your personalized pain relief formula. I do not recommend that you review day seven until you have completed today's program. There is always a tendency to go slightly faster than is recommended, especially when you are probably beginning to experience pain relief benefits from the first five days.

Daily Review.

This will be your last daily review, since on day seven I'm going to be presenting you with something different. By now you should be answering yes to all of the statements with almost no need for review.

Here is your final review. Answer yes or no to each statement.

1. Does the pain control object have to be used over and over to maintain control of the pain object?

2. Am I capable of using the personalized pain relief formula to reduce and control the pain?

At this time I am going to ask you to go back to the

first five days and repeat the daily reviews. I have full
confidence that you have been able to answer most or all
of these questions with a resounding *yes*! But if any statements are unclear, reread that section, and change the no
to a yes.

Today's Pain Relief Formula.

Your Personalized Pain Relief
Formula—Part Two

The Basics.

Only one more day to go and you will have your finalized
personalized pain relief formula. You have worked hard
up to this point, so don't get ahead of yourself. Slow,
steady, and even pacing will always be to your benefit.

Your personalized pain relief formula—part two will incorporate for the first time your pain segment. At the end
of each pain segment is a formula statement which is to
be included in your personalized pain relief formula. In
today's instructions you will be given the appropriate place
for insertion of your formula statement.

I suggest that you write your formula statement on a
piece of paper and then commit it to memory, since you
will be using it throughout today's sessions.

Goals.

The personalized pain relief formula—part two will accomplish the following:

It will intensify your pain control skills.

It will combine pain relief imagery with your formula statement.

It will shorten the activation time to under thirty seconds.

Instructions.

Follow today's instructions carefully, reading them over at least twice prior to beginning. At this point you should have your pain relief formula statement memorized.

With your eyes open, inhale deeply through your nose and exhale slowly through your mouth.

Visualize your pain control object destroying your pain object.

(*Note:* Always make sure to use the pain control color and pain color.)

Repeat your pain relief statement silently to yourself five times. Example:
I am in control of my _____ (insert pain site or description as found in the pain segment)

Again, visualize your pain control object attacking the pain object.

Repeat your pain relief formula statement five times to yourself silently.

Continue alternating your mental visualization with silent repetition of your pain relief formula statement.

Take a deep breath, let it out slowly, and stretch your arms and legs.

Today's Practice

Morning Session.

TIME = Twenty minutes

REPETITIONS = Repeat formula in four complete segments during this twenty-minute session. Start and terminate your personalized pain relief formula—part two with pain relief formula statement every five minutes (four complete segments during your twenty-minute session).

FORMAT: Perform your personalized pain relief formula—part two with the pain relief formula statement.

Daily Sessions.

TIME = Twenty to thirty seconds

REPETITIONS = Twice every hour from 9:00 A.M. to 6:00 P.M. Try to practice more than twice an hour but do not abbreviate the formula. Because you are going to use your personalized pain relief formula—part two with the pain relief formula statement, allow thirty seconds to complete the entire formula. Do not cut it short or modify it.

FORMAT:

With your eyes open, take one pain relief breath.

Visualize your pain control object attacking the pain object.

Repeat your pain relief formula statement silently to yourself twice.

Visualize your pain control object attacking your pain object.

Take a deep breath, let it out slowly, and gently stretch your arms and legs.

Evening Session.

TIME = Twenty minutes

REPETITIONS: See below

For this evening session, your time will be approximately

twenty minutes; but during that time period you are to practice the daily session format just presented under the heading *Daily Sessions*. I realize you will not be able to complete the personalized pain relief formula—part two with the pain relief formula statement every thirty seconds for twenty minutes. This would be tremendously fatiguing and very difficult to accomplish. When you practice for tonight's session, keep each complete segment to thirty seconds or less and take a short break (approximately two minutes) between each.

Day Six in Review

You are now at a point where your formula is completed in thirty seconds or less. I do not expect that you will be completely proficient in its execution, nor will you find each thirty-second segment to be an improvement upon the last. You can only move just so fast.

Following completion of your evening session, try to continue practicing in thirty-second segments at least twice every hour, with your last thirty-second segment performed while you are in bed, just prior to falling asleep.

Today you have learned:

To integrate your pain relief formula statement with your personalized pain relief formula—part two

To utilize the complete formula in thirty seconds or less

A Preview of Day Seven.

Day seven is just around the corner, and with it the final building block of your seven-day pain relief program. Tomorrow's design and requirements will be different from those of the previous six days, and therefore I advise you to take the time now to review day seven.

Day Seven

Introduction.

Today is the last day of the intensive seven-day part of the Scottsdale Pain Relief Program. Tomorrow you will begin the Lifetime Maintenance Program, and the excitement has just begun. At this point I think it is important to let you know that if you are reading these sentences after completing six days of the program, then you need to congratulate yourself on a task that has been difficult, demanding, and possibly frustrating at times. If you can complete the six days (there is no reason why you can't) by using your personalized pain relief formula, then you can continue to improve and expand your ability to gain pain relief, retake control of your emotions, and begin enjoying life.

At this point in the program, you should also be noticing some of the positive factors that your emotions are beginning to create. People may comment to you that you seem like a changed person, or that something is different about you. Don't be bashful and deny yourself these compliments. Take them; you earned each and every word of praise.

Daily Review.

Your daily review for today will consist of rereading your pain segment in chapter three and completely reviewing the Lifetime Maintenance Program in part three.

Today's Pain Relief Formula.

The Personalized Pain Relief Formula

The Basics.

Today's formula represents a culmination of all six days of intensive application and practice. The personalized pain relief formula combines pain relief breathing, the pain relief scan, pain control objects, pain control color, pain objects, pain color, and your pain relief formula statement. All of these techniques are now combined into one simple, effective, and powerful formula.

You have yet to reach a point where your body and mind work together automatically to initiate the formula, and therefore you will have to continue practicing on a daily basis throughout the course of the Lifetime Maintenance Program. This may seem like a never-ending task, but once you have become proficient at using your pain relief formula, you will only be using minutes each day for continued pain relief and emotion-stabilizing benefits.

Goals.

Today's goal can be simply stated:

To activate the complete personalized pain relief formula anytime, anywhere, and under any circumstances

Instructions.

As a little surprise for you, today there will be no morning session, daily session, or evening session. You are to begin using the personalized pain relief formula on a twice-hourly basis from the time you awaken to the time you go to sleep. This might seem like a tremendous amount of practice, but at this time in the program, you should be prepared for a commitment of this magnitude and encouraged by the fact that each practice session will take no longer than thirty seconds for completion.

If you awaken at 6:00 A.M. and go to sleep at 10:00 P.M., this represents sixteen hours of twice-hourly practice, or thirty-two sessions. The total required practice time during one complete day will be *sixteen minutes*. One minute per hour, sixteen minutes per day, is not an exorbitant price to pay for pain relief and emotional stability.

Follow the instructions carefully, and read them over twice before beginning your day.

Take one pain relief breath.

Visualize your pain control object attacking your pain object.

Silently repeat your pain relief statement (once).

Take a deep breath, and let it out slowly, flexing your arms and legs.

At this point in the program, you will have the choice of practicing with your eyes open or closed. Most people find it preferable to practice with their eyes closed while lying in bed or just prior to going to sleep. In fact, most patients report an enhanced ability to sleep with a prolonged and deeper sleep pattern if they practice their personalized pain relief formula just prior to attempting sleep.

Today's Practice

TIME = Thirty seconds per session

REPETITIONS = Twice every hour from awakening in the morning until going to sleep at night

FORMAT: The complete personalized pain relief formula

The Final Day in Review

Twice an hour every hour seems like a lot, but in reality it's a small price to pay for lifetime benefits, some of which you have already begun to experience. Whenever you practice your personalized pain relief formula, use it completely. Do not abbreviate it or take any shortcuts.

If you want to use the formula more than twice an hour, please do so. Be innovative and experiment with its use. For instance, if you are feeling stressed by a particularly difficult meeting, then use the formula with your eyes open to reduce stress and prevent a stress/pain buildup. No one will realize you are using the formula. The more you experiment with its use under varying situations and circumstances, the more proficient you will become, with a proportional gain in confidence as you experience the positive results.

The Final Assignment.

The final assignment for the seven-day program will be to read part three of the book.

Part Three

The seven-day program is finished but not forgotten. I strongly encourage you to refer to any part of the seven-day program as often as you feel the need to review. This also applies to any of the sections in part one. Since you are not an inanimate object but a constantly changing organism within an ever-changing environment, you will need to refresh your memory at times or reread parts of the book and apply them to new situations.

Part three will contain your Lifetime Maintenance Program and the chapters, *Eat, Sleep, Be Merry, and Control Your Pain* and *A Prescription for Living.*

When you suffer from chronic pain, it affects your entire lifestyle. Because you are not just a back injury, a migraine headache, or an arthritic hand but a fully functioning individual who has a chronic pain problem, the Lifetime Maintenance Program has been designed specifically to have a spillover effect. Typical patient responses best demonstrate how the Scottsdale Pain Relief Program will affect positively all areas of your life.

"When I finished the seven-day part, I was flying high. For the first time in three years I could sit long enough to go to the movies with my family. They said I was not a stranger anymore."

—BILL P.

"Every day I was depressed by the thought of another day of headaches. I know people didn't like me anymore and I didn't like myself. The program taught me how to stop the headaches and I can now look at myself in the mirror and smile."

—LINDA M.

"Some days I would sit and plan how to kill myself. The pain was like a gun pointed at my head all the time. I went through the pain program. The pain is still there but much less and I don't feel like killing myself. I'm even thinking about the future. I didn't think I had one before."

—GARY K.

You can see from these comments that the techniques you have learned and the foundation of knowledge you have gained will be a very powerful tool to help you improve the quality of your life. As with any tool, it has no function unless you pick it up, learn how to use it, and actually apply it. As you move through the chapters in part three, constantly challenge yourself by asking how the information presented to you may be applied to you as a whole, fully functioning person.

Chapter Five

The Lifetime Maintenance Program

In the Scottsdale Pain Relief Program there are three distinct points of celebration: the first, when you successfully complete the intensive seven-day program; the second, when you begin the Lifetime Maintenance Program; and the third, the continuous celebration each and every day you use the pain relief formulas to regain dignity in your life.

By now you have proven your commitment and desire for pain control to a very important person: yourself. If you let that commitment waiver for even one day, you will pay a price.

"I was so busy today I completely forgot."

"I had the flu. You can't expect me to practice."

"I was doing so well, a few days off seemed like an appropriate reward."

If you were with me, I would ask you what is wrong with the statements you have just read. I hope you would look concerned and note how the people behind the statements were deceiving themselves. Your comment would come out this way:

> When I started the program, you let me know right off about the commitment needed to be successful. I remember that every day of the seven-day program you reinforced the idea of a maintenance program only being as good as an individual's ability to practice every day; and I remember the two enemies—discouragement, which could lead to prematurely stopping the program, and overconfidence, which could lead to the erroneous conclusion that once you experience successful pain relief, practice is no longer necessary.

If you have come this far, why ruin your achievements by becoming overconfident, lazy, or procrastinating?

Help! I'm Being Held Prisoner by My Pain.

There are no bars, no guards, and no high walls with spotlights, but just as surely as if you were in prison, you could experience your pain becoming a life sentence with no parole. You've already gone past the stage of expectation (that your pain will disappear) and into the stage of despair (thinking, I may have to live like this for the rest of my life).

Although the pain is the gatekeeper, you may now make

the decision to apply for a lifetime parole. The seven-day program was simply the parole application process; now that you have successfully completed that test, it will be up to you to make a decision regarding the Lifetime Maintenance Program. Once you make the decision to leave your pain prison, you will only return if you stop practicing and working every day toward pain relief. Unfortunately, your cell will never be occupied by anyone else and will always be awaiting your return should you fail in your Lifetime Maintenance Program.

The comparison might sound somewhat drastic, but for anyone who has suffered from a chronic pain syndrome for more than nine months, it can feel as though you are a prisoner of your pain.

Strength in Numbers.

Yes, you can form a maintenance group. There are times when several people independently have completed the seven-day program and, for additional support, have developed a group approach to implementing the maintenance program. You do not have to begin a group that only sticks to the maintenance design I will present here.

Not everyone in the group needs to have the same type of pain, but it might help, especially when identifying with each other's special needs or difficulties.

Here's an example of how one person developed and implemented a maintenance group.

Sharon's Group

Sharon M. suffers from rheumatoid arthritis. Her story was the same as literally millions of others, until she participated in the Scottsdale Pain Relief Program. When she completed the program, she was not pain-free, but she had reduced certain aspects of her discomfort to a tolerable level. She had increased her daily activities and was now doing volunteer work. She was challenging life again.

As she began the Lifetime Maintenance Program, Sharon decided to contact other people who had just completed the seven-day program. Since Sharon had first heard about the program during a seminar I gave to an arthritis self-help group, she knew at least six other people at approximately the same stage of the Scottsdale Pain Relief Program.

She took the risk and called the people, inviting them over to her house on a Tuesday night with the idea of discussing their progress and exchanging ideas. To her surprise and pleasure, five out of the six attended the first meeting. After getting to know each other, they proceeded to have a lively discussion regarding their experiences with the program. Each person told a similar story, with some variations. Soon it was late and they decided to meet again in two weeks at one of the other people's houses.

Two years have passed since the initial meeting at Sharon's house, and the group still meets on a monthly basis. They have become more than good friends, for they share the continued dedication never to let pain ruin their lives again. I have been invited to speak to their group informally on at least three occasions, and each time I have come away with excellent ideas and suggestions. Whenever people contact me about starting a group, I give them Sharon's name and the next thing I know, I'm being invited to speak to a new group. To watch the beginning of a new group is an exciting experience.

Why Form a Group?

Several important growth factors may be germinated through maintenance groups. The fellowship, support, and caring provided by these groups can be immensely helpful when a member's condition deteriorates even while they are using the program to control the pain.

STARTING A GROUP. If you want to start your own maintenance group, follow these simple suggestions and you may find a very pleasant and enriching experience just around the corner.

Contact the prospective people for your group and arrange for the first meeting.

Try to limit your group size to six or less.

Be sure all group participants have completed successfully the seven-day program.

The Lifetime Maintenance Program Explained.

The Lifetime Maintenance Program is exactly what its name implies. This is the program to follow for the rest of your life. Before proceeding any further, you need to do two things:

1. Thoroughly read chapter six.

2. Go to chapter three, pick the pain segment that applies to your specific discomfort, and review that segment completely.

In chapter seven, you will be given a prescription for living.

By completing both of these requirements, you will gain a better understanding of additional methods for controlling your pain. All of the techniques and suggestions that are presented to you are extremely important and should not be taken lightly. Although your personalized pain relief formula will be the most powerful tool in the ongoing effort to maintain pain relief, the suggestions provided to you in chapter six and the pain segment will add to your success.

Why Activities?

During the course of your seven-day program, you will expend significant effort toward re-educating your body/mind connection to decrease pain, increase pain tolerance, and help you obtain an emotional facelift.

Activity and exercise on a daily basis send a message to your brain that is positive in nature. It will respond with the production of natural chemicals that serve as anti-depression and antianxiety substances. The runner's high is not the sole property of world-class athletes. Research has shown that any activity that elevates the heart rate and lasts for from twelve to fifteen minutes will cause the production of these internal emotion stabilizers.

Your Benefits.

By participating in a daily activity program, you will soon begin to experience these very pleasant, rewarding benefits:

Increased muscular strength

Increased muscular endurance

Increased flexibility

Increased blood flow to the muscles

Increased elimination of waste materials from the muscles

Increased ability to deal with stress

Increased positive self-image

Increased capacity for stretching

Increased cardiopulmonary fitness

Increased self-confidence

Increased energy

Of course you will not benefit from all of these positive results the first time you participate in your daily activity. It usually takes at least two or three weeks before you begin to notice significant, positive changes, but you have to start the ball rolling on day one of the seven-day program.

The Best Five Exercises

Before I determined the top five exercises for people with chronic pain problems, I consulted with exercise physiologists, physicians of all and varied specialties, physical therapists, and physical fitness coaches.

Each specialist was asked to rate the activity based upon several factors: potential for injury, potential for reinjury, cardiovascular benefits, ease of application, cost-effectiveness, and musculoskeletal benefits. After compiling all of the data, the top five factors were:

Walking

Stationary exercycle

Low impact aerobics

Swimming

Biking

In your search for the appropriate exercise, please consider one of the above as a possible first choice.

(*Note:* After you choose any activity, be sure to consult your physician and obtain his approval.)

Setting Up the
Exercise/Activity Program

After you have approval from your physician, it is time to begin your exercise/activity program. Whichever exercise/activity you select, there are some ground rules you should always observe:

1. Participate in your exercise/activity program at least once a day. Twice a day will not hurt, but you should be careful not to overdo it. *Never* sacrifice other parts of your seven-day program for an extra exercise/activity period.

2. The exercise/activity program should be performed *every* day. No excuses!

3. When you perform any stretching exercise, use a firm yet comfortable surface.

4. Pay careful attention to your body position at all times.

5. Pace yourself correctly. You should never be in a race to finish.

6. Clothing should be loose and comfortable. If your exercise/activity program involves walking or use of an exercycle, invest in a good pair of jogging, walking, or aerobic shoes.

7. Do not continue your exercise/activity periods if you experience a steady increase in pain.

Exercise/Activity Pitfalls to Avoid.

1. Pick an exercise/activity program that is compatible with your age, physical capacities, and pain situation. Refer to the section in this chapter on making your exercise/activity choice, which will provide you with a list of recommended activities for various physical conditions.

2. Start slowly and increase gradually. If you choose a walking program, for example, don't become involved with a neighbor who has been walking for three years and invites you out for a three-mile journey on your first attempt.

3. Don't hesitate to change any activity that prompts an increase in your pain response or that you find unsatisfactory for other reasons such as weather or safety.

4. Don't vary your exercise/activity times. Be consistent. Let a positive habit form by setting aside a specific time each day.

High-Risk Activities

If you have a muscle, ligament, or bone condition, then it will be important for you to avoid certain types of activities. Although you might have participated in these activities before your injury occurred or your condition began, you will no longer be able to pursue them safely without significantly increasing the risk of reinjury or even new injury due to your present physical condition. Use common sense, and if that voice inside tells you not to participate, by all means *listen*. I have listed some of these activities with a brief explanation:

1. *Football, basketball, and baseball.* Because they involve twisting, jarring movements, jumping, bending, and contact with other players, these sports are potentially hazardous for a weak back or neck.

2. *Bowling.* This activity can easily aggravate back or neck problems, since you lift a heavy weight while twisting and bending your upper body.

3. *Weight lifting.* Lifting free (loose) weights can put tremendous amounts of stress on the musculoskeletal system. If you exercise at a health spa with Nautilus-type equipment, it is absolutely essential that you make sure the person designing your exercise program is aware of your pain problem and is qualified to design a program that will not reinjure you.

4. *Tennis and Other Racquet Sports.* These sports can strain the back because of their twisting and quick stop-go movements added to the pounding shock of the hard court.

5. *Golf.* A recent survey found that twenty-five percent of all golf pros suffer from low back injuries. The twisting movement of the swing, constant bending to tee the ball or remove the ball from the cup, and prolonged putting or driving practice may lead to a back reinjury.

Activities Your Body Will Like.

Just because you have an injury or pain condition, there is no reason why you cannot participate in enjoyable activities. Certain activities not only provide excellent cardiovascular conditioning, muscle toning, and positive emotional responses, but they are also excellent for anyone with a pain condition.

1. *Swimming.* This is the best sport for relieving musculoskeletal pain, since the water supports the spine, thus relieving pressure on it. It also helps tone and stretch key muscles. The backstroke and the sidestroke are best for the back, legs, arms, shoulders, and hips. Avoid the butterfly and the breaststroke, which cause you to arch your back.

2. *Cycling.* This is excellent aerobic exercise if you have pain problems, provided you maintain an upright position. It is not recommended for arthritis, however, so instead use a stationary exercycle.

3. *Walking.* This is the perfect exercise for promoting a healthy body/mind. According to the Swedish back expert Dr. Alf Nachemson, walking puts less strain on the spine than does unsupported sitting, and only a little more than plain standing. You may begin a walking program with no practice, and you need no special equipment except for good shoes.

Your Personal Activity Program

Repetitive daily activity is an integral part of the Scottsdale Pain Relief Program. You need to perform your personal activity program at least once a day, every day. To break up any boredom, I always recommend at least two activities that can be alternated or varied.

(*Note:* Prior to beginning any physical activity program, you should obtain the approval of your physician. Your doctor may provide you with suggestions for various activities based upon your physical condition.)

Exercise / Activity Program.

You are to continue your activity on a once-daily basis. Maintain a schedule that allows you to participate in the activity at the same time each day. Consistency leads to increased chances for success.

If you begin to tire of your activity/exercise, then begin developing a substitute for your primary interest. For example, many of my patients begin a walking program and after several months substitute a few times a week with swimming. This provides for an extremely well-rounded approach to your exercise/activity program. The program may be divided in the following manner:

Walking—Monday, Wednesday, Friday, Saturday, and Sunday

Swimming—Tuesday and Thursday

You may alternate among two or three activities, just as long as you perform them on a daily basis, without fail.

Your Personalized Pain Relief Formula.

On day seven of the program, you developed your personalized pain relief formula. This short version allowed you to complete the entire formula in from thirty to forty seconds. I asked you to practice on an every-thirty-minutes basis. The every-thirty-minutes practice schedule will be continued, but within three weeks you will already begin to notice definite changes. As you use the pain relief breathing, your mind will begin to activate the personalized pain relief formula before you can actually begin to use the autogenic pain relief phrases or the pain control imagery. A positive habit of pain relief will be formed and begin to be activated on an automatic basis.

Once the pain relief reaction becomes automatic, you will find it being activated not only for your pain but for any part of the emotional fallout, which has been discussed earlier. When the personalized pain relief formula is activated automatically for emotions, it becomes an emotion-stabilizing formula. The diagram below presents the chain reaction that occurs with continuous practice during the Lifetime Maintenance Program.

Pain → *Personalized* → *Decreased* → *Activation* → *Decreased*
   Pain Relief   *Pain*   *of Automatic*   *Emotional*
   Formula   *Emotion-*   *Distress*
            Stabilizing
            Formula

Summary.

You know how to use your personalized pain relief formula not only for pain but as an emotion-stabilizing formula. In chapter six you are going to learn how food and sleep can affect your pain. Read the chapter carefully, for the information contained within it is absolutely essential for continued success in the Lifetime Maintenance Program.

Chapter Six

Eat, Sleep, Be Merry, and Control Your Pain

Your body is a tremendously complicated electrochemical machine that needs to be fueled. I have already shown you how stress can directly affect your pain by increasing it and decreasing your emotional resilience. What we have not discussed is the fact that chronic pain, through its stress response, can cause the body to burn a significant amount of energy, thus creating a very high demand for the proper intake of food. A balanced diet is extremely important for anyone who is suffering from pain.

During the past several years, there have been reports of special diets that cause a decrease in pain. When most of these diets are explored in depth, however, I have found that the major component is a healthy balance of proteins, carbohydrates, and fats.

There are certain foods that may contribute to your discomfort through allergic or physiological reactions. This problem has been dealt with in the section on how foods feed your pain in this chapter.

(*Note:* Maintaining a correct balance of proteins, carbohydrates, and fats in your food intake is of extreme importance. Check with your physician about the correct combination for you.)

Serotonin—A Crucial Link.

Serotonin is manufactured naturally within the brain and serves as a neurotransmitter, facilitating the flow of messages within the body's network of nerves. The appropriate production of serotonin has been linked to better sleep, calmer moods, increased energy levels, and control over appetite. It is a key ingredient in the pain response mechanism.

Before delving more completely into serotonin and its link to pain, let's take a moment and discuss exactly what serotonin's function is within the human body. Serotonin, which has been classified as a neurotransmitter, is released at the neurons (nerve fiber endings) and helps the nerve impulses cross the synaptic gap between two neurons.

Serotonin is a neurotransmitter that is derived from the essential amino acid tryptophan and is found in the blood, most nerve cells, and other body tissues. Tryptophan is a specific nutrient that is derived from certain protein foods; it may be purchased over the counter in tablet form. If you follow any good, healthy diet that allows for a proper balance of proteins, carbohydrates, and fats, you will help to insure that an adequate level of tryptophan is produced by the brain and therefore provide for adequate levels of serotonin.

Serotonin and the Pain Threshold.

Recent scientific studies have indicated that decreased levels of serotonin in the blood and tissue can cause people to have a lower tolerance for pain. When their serotonin level is appropriate, people will have an adequate ability to utilize the body's built-in painkillers, allowing them to work adequately toward decreasing the body's pain. When the body's serotonin level is low or depleted, pain you normally would have been able to ignore becomes greater both in terms of when you notice it and when it becomes intolerable.

(*Note:* Lower levels of tryptophan lead to decreased serotonin production within the brain and cause an increased sensitivity to pain and decreased ability to produce the body's internal painkillers.)

Maintaining Serotonin Levels.

We have seen that the body's production of serotonin is linked directly to the production of the amino acid tryptophan. Remember that amino acids occur naturally in plant and animal tissues and serve both as a built-in block of protein molecules (serotonin) and as some of the body's built-in painkillers (endorphins, enkephalins). Amino acids must be obtained from foods or supplements. The human body synthesizes many amino acids from the food sources in your diet.

If serotonin is responsible for endorphins and enkephalins, which are found in the brain areas and produce analgesia (pain relief), and it acts to switch on and off neurons involved in pain control, then having appropriate levels of serotonin to insure the proper transmission of signals that increase the body's production of natural pain killers is obviously essential.

Increased Pain Threshold—A Partial Answer.

If we are able to increase our pain threshold, then the point at which we will notice pain is increased and we are able to tolerate greater degrees of pain without the devastating physical and emotional aftereffects. Increased pain threshold is only one part of the answer, but it does play a role in the total Lifetime Maintenance Program. By eating correctly through a well-balanced diet, we can insure an adequate production of tryptophan and thus create an environment for appropriate serotonin production. Some scientists and doctors have advocated the supplementation of tryptophan through tablets. I would recommend consulting your physician before trying this. Although tryptophan has been judged safe enough for over-the-counter administration, it is always best to check with your physician. Serotonin cannot be obtained in supplemental form, so don't go to your favorite pharmacist and ask him for a serotonin pill.

Scientific research has shown one other way in which serotonin production is increased within the human body, and that is through exercise. Earlier we discussed the beneficial aspects to exercising and elevating the heart rate and, therefore, increasing the body's production of serotonin which not only affects the body's level of pain threshold but serves as a natural antidepressant (the runner's high).

Keeping You Safe.

It is interesting to note that serotonin, endorphins, and enkephalins all serve to increase our ability to withstand pain and help achieve a greater degree of emotional stability without removing pain perception. Since pain is the body's warning signal, it would be detrimental to our health if the body could no longer provide us an alarm system indicating a body malfunction.

None of the internally produced painkillers will remove the body's ability to signal the alarm relating to body malfunction.

A Stuck Signal.

Unfortunately, anyone who experiences chronic pain has a horn which is stuck and, therefore, the warning signal actually becomes an irritant. The body's built-in chemicals that are facilitated through proper diet and appropriate food intake will facilitate natural chemical balance and enhance your internal abilities to obtain control over your pain through the Scottsdale Pain Relief Program.

The Proper Food Intake.

Obtaining information regarding the appropriate intake of protein, carbohydrates, and fats is a simple matter of contacting your physician, the American Heart Association, the local YMCA, or numerous other organizations who will gladly provide you with appropriate diets. If you have any difficulty obtaining this information, go to your local hospital and ask to speak with the nutritionist. I am sure he or she would be happy to provide you with additional sources regarding safe and appropriate diet information.

The Pain of Eating Poorly.

A report in the June 1983 issue of the *Journal of Surgery* directs attention to a correlation between good nutrition and increased functioning of the body's immune, healing, and pain reduction systems. Since we know that pain can suppress the body's immune system (the ability to fight disease and repair itself), we must not allow a suppression in the immune system by insuring proper nutrition to maintain the body's ability to tolerate pain as effectively as possible.

How Food Feeds Your Pain.

Pain has a voracious appetite and likes to be fed. We have seen how we might feed pain from a physical and emotional standpoint. Now you will learn how not to help your pain by eating foods that may cause an increase in discomfort.

Before telling you what you should or should not eat, I need to emphasize the importance of eating meals at regular times and not overeating—especially when you're experiencing pain or the emotional fallout from pain increases.

Pain Triggers.

Most research regarding the role of certain foods, liquids, and chemical substances as triggers for pain has been limited to headaches. I have found during the course of my practice that making anyone who suffers from pain aware of food triggers often will have a beneficial effect upon the individual's particular pain response.

If you suffer from headaches, absolutely avoid the triggers. If you are experiencing other types of pain, try eliminating these substances and judge for yourself whether or not they have an effect on your pain response.

Pain Triggers

Cheeses, such as Brie, Gruyère, and cheddar (natural and aged and high in tyramine content which may cause vascular changes and trigger headaches)

Chocolate milk

Smoked and processed meats such as hot dogs, bologna, and sausage

Peanut butter

Beer

Seeds such as sunflower or pumpkin

Monosodium glutamate (MSG) flavoring (found in meat tenderizers and Chinese cooking)

Soft drinks containing caffeine

Chocolate

Coffee

(In excess) bananas, citrus fruits, and yeast extracts

Pickled and marinated food

In the list of pain triggers I have tried to include the major offenders and instigators of pain. In the past whenever I have presented such a list to patients, I could have almost guaranteed that someone was going to come up and say something like "lamb chops caused my joints to ache." Because each of us is an individually functioning system in our environment, certain foods or substances not listed may cause you an increase in pain or may actually trigger the onset of discomfort. If you notice that each time you eat a particular food it is followed by either the onset of pain or increased pain, then by all means eliminate that item to determine if you have a pain trigger I have not discussed. You should also be aware of the fact that since we are constantly changing systems, a pain trigger that did not bother you five years ago may become a pain trigger now or in the future. Your constant evaluation of possible pain triggers will be a necessity for your Lifetime Maintenance Program.

Pick and Choose.

Controlling the amount that we eat is difficult enough, but trying to eliminate all of the items listed at one time would be very difficult. While trying to avoid most items on the list, be aware of any changes in your pain patterns that may occur when you eliminate a particular item (especially if you are a headache sufferer). If you go to a Chinese restaurant, ask for dishes without MSG. Be aware that eliminating these items from your diet should take place over an extended period of time. Stopping your intake of peanut butter for two days, for instance, is likely to have little effect upon your pain. Common sense will also tell you that if you only eat chocolate once every three weeks and you have headaches four times weekly, the chance that the chocolate is a trigger for your headaches is slight.

Sleep—A Crucial Element.

"Ah, ah, if only I could get a decent night's sleep. I can't remember the last time I slept through the whole night."

"I can't seem to turn off my mind when I try and go to sleep. All that happens is that I lie there and toss and turn, and toss and turn."

For anyone who has experienced pain, obtaining a good night's sleep is a goal worth its weight in gold. During sleep the body rebuilds, recuperates, and prepares you for the following day. If your sleep cycle becomes disrupted for even two or three days, the body's ability to produce its own built-in painkillers becomes impaired. Additionally, when you lose sleep there's a greater susceptibility to depression. If you don't believe me, take a look at how you or anyone you know reacts when not sleeping well for two or three days. You will notice the appearance of depressive-type symptoms.

I mentioned earlier in this chapter the beneficial effect that proper diet will have on the production of tryptophan, which in essence will help facilitate increased levels of the neurotransmitter serotonin. We took a look at serotonin's beneficial effect of increasing your ability to withstand higher degrees of pain. Besides its effect on pain, the production of serotonin is an ingredient to facilitate quicker and longer sleep patterns.

The Warm Glass of Milk.

Most of us remember grandmother talking about having a warm glass of milk before bedtime to insure a good night's sleep. Well, this wasn't just an old wives' tale; research has found that having a warm glass of milk actually stimulates increased tryptophan production in the brain and thus enhances the use of serotonin.

Do's and Don't's.

Here are some do's and don't's to help you obtain a better night's sleep and awaken more refreshed and better able to use your personalized pain relief formula.

Don't's

Don't eat a large meal within three hours of planning to go to sleep

Don't perform your exercise/activity program within an hour of going to sleep

Don't take over-the-counter sleeping medications

Don't take anyone else's sleep medication without first checking with your physician

Don't lie in bed trying to organize your tomorrows

Don't concentrate on disturbing thoughts prior to attempting sleep

Do, Do, Do . . .

Do make sure that your bed is appropriate if you have a neuromuscular pain problem

Do use your personalized pain relief formula once you are lying in bed, as a method for relaxing your body and inducing sleep

Do use the pain relief scan when you first lie down in bed to insure the release of muscular tension

Do consult your physician if your sleep difficulties last longer than one week

Summary.

I have found, through my years of care and treatment involving pain, that one of the key statements of advice I can give is to use common sense at all times. Don't become involved in fad diets or remedies. A good, nutritious diet and appropriate sleep will serve as important ingredients for your success within the Lifetime Maintenance Program.

Chapter Seven

A Prescription
for Living

Although each chapter of the Scottsdale Pain Relief Program is of equal importance, this chapter will help you to set and firm your course of success in utilizing the Lifetime Maintenance Program.

Read each section carefully (reviewing the chapter more than once will be beneficial). If you are not sure whether a section applies to your pattern of behavior or coping style, ask your spouse or another person who knows you to give you his or her honest opinion. Before asking for anyone's opinion, let the person read this chapter in its entirety.

A Word Before You Start.

Always be open to discovering and learning from all aspects of your emotional and physical behavior. Remember, the main objective of this chapter is to help you extinguish the behaviors that might reinforce your pain and prevent success in the Lifetime Maintenance Program.

Daily Exercise / Activity.

Keep up the good work. If there has been any difficulty in performing your activity, evaluate your daily schedule and make any appropriate adjustments. Don't wait until tomorrow.

Pain Relief Thinking

As you think, you are. Never has a truer statement been spoken. If all you think of is pain and if your past, present, and future revolves around pain, then your pain will be reinforced. The more you focus on your pain, the less effective the pain relief formulas will be in utilizing your body's built-in painkillers to provide you with relief.

As with everything in the Scottsdale Pain Relief Program, pain relief thinking will take practice, but after a relatively short time the habit pattern will be formed. Follow these simple instructions and by the end of day seven pain relief thinking will have become an important tool you can use for success in your battle with pain.

Whenever you have a negative pain thought (thinking about pain while using the pain relief formula or pain relief breathing should not be considered neg-

ative) consciously think to yourself the words I am in control.

The words I am in control *repeated silently to yourself will block the pain thought and will become an appropriate linking mechanism for automatic activation of your personal pain relief formula.*

At first you will have to repeat the phrase I am in control *from three to five times to block effectively the negative pain thought. After practicing, you will find that the phrase* I am in control *will become automatic, short-circuiting the negative pain response.*

Here are some samples of negative pain responses that need to be removed.

"I am getting discouraged about my pain."

"My pain will probably be worse tomorrow."

"The weather is making my pain greater."

"I don't think I'll be able to go because of my pain."

"My pain will probably be worse today."

"I'll never feel better!"

Mind Over Emotions

As you are now aware, your emotions play a significant role in your chronic pain complex. The mind-over-emotions part of the pain relief statement is designed specifically to help you gain the greatest degree of control over emotions such as depression, anxiety, frustration, irritability, and anger, which all serve to pump up your pain. You are going to be requesting your mind and body to work together as a team not only to identify but also to control any emotions that interfere with your ability for pain relief.

Always include the pain relief statement as part of the personalized pain relief formula. You may want to use some of the other pain relief statements found in chapter three.

Sexual Activity and Pain.

"Not tonight, I've got a headache."

How many times have we heard that famous statement on television or in the movies? It's the age-old excuse. It never seems to go out of style.

Participating in sexual activity is of great concern to anyone who has suffered a back injury. Most of the time, advice is very short, nondescriptive, and possibly damaging ("If it hurts, stop."). So what happens to the person with a back injury? The first time sexual relations are attempted and pain is experienced, activity has to stop. A man will develop secondary impotency due to the anxiety and anticipation about the increase in pain. This scenario is similar to the one experienced by post-heart attack victims, when the doctor tells them that sexual activity is just fine ("but don't get too excited").

Not an Excuse.

Don't allow your pain to be an excuse for avoiding sexual activity. If you develop an excuse mechanism by blaming your pain, then you may find your body and mind working together to increase pain and thus present you with a more justifiable excuse.

Pain Relief.

Recent studies have both indicated and verified that the body increases the production of endogenous circulating opioids (including endorphins) as a result of sexual stimulation. During the past several years, for example, articles have appeared in newspapers and magazines relating to research that suggested that sexual activity could modify the pain of arthritis.

Common Sense.

When in doubt, use common sense.

Be open to discussing any fears or apprehensions you may have with your sexual partner. Openness and honesty will go a long way toward the development of gratifying sexual activity that will not increase significantly your level of discomfort and, in fact, may actually aid in your pain relief.

Positive Pain Relief Addiction

"I'm pleased to inform you of your pending addiction to the Scottsdale Pain Relief Program."

Sound strange? Of course it does, especially since anyone who has been on (narcotic) pain relief medication is keenly aware of that devastating word *addiction*. Heroin users become addicted; cocaine users become addicted; alcoholics become addicted. All of these addictions have negative consequences.

Now I'm telling you about the *positive* addiction to the Scottsdale Pain Relief Program.

I'm sure many of you have experienced the frustration of sitting in your doctor's examining room with continuing complaints of pain and hearing him say, "I really can't give you any more medication because I think you are becoming addicted." Unfortunately no alternative is provided, which leaves you in a situation where you are counting your pills, going to other doctors for medication (doctor shopping), or even showing up at your local emergency room and presenting the right number of symptoms to get the right medication.

Are You Positively Addicted?

You know you are positively addicted when the following events happen:

You look forward to your exercise/activity program.

Your postactivity glow (feelings of well-being and calmness) lasts for more than twenty minutes.

You practice your pain relief formula more than required.

The major drawback to positive addiction can be found if you miss more than one day of activities. The withdrawal symptoms that you will experience are similar to those of nicotine, caffeine, or even medication. Once your body becomes accustomed to the natural chemical production fostered by consistent activity, then you are hooked on positive addiction.

Stress

The time has come for me to tell you about a very serious topic and something that needs to be dealt with immediately. Now that you have completed the seven-day program, you probably will have experienced positive outcomes to pain relief and increased emotional control. You will have attained your personalized pain relief formula and be able to activate it in thirty-to-forty-five seconds or less any time or any place you desire. You have worked extremely hard and made a commitment for those seven days; but upon completion of the program, some people fall into a trap of becoming complacent. I have been providing you with information every day that I am going to ask you to rely upon in the Lifetime Maintenance Program. There are several factors that may cause problems or interfere with successful maintenance. Stress is one of them, and so you need to start developing the ability to cope with it.

What Is Stress?

Think for a minute about what the word *stress* means to you. What I know for certain is that no matter how many people I ask about stress and what it means to them, I may get many different answers. Most people will be consistent in one response: Stress isn't good for you, but it's a fact of life. Stress has become the buzzword of the 1980s and in all likelihood will continue that way into the 1990s. This infamous word has been blamed for everything from the sinking of the Titanic to tension in Soviet-American relations—rightly so, since stress does play a significant role in all of our daily lives and—most important—our health.

Stress, in its most basic form, is the way you react—physically and emotionally—to pain.

Positive and Negative Stress.

Stress comes in two varieties: positive and negative. Not all stress is bad, but some stress can be linked directly to devastating diseases such as cancer. The body's immune system becomes depleted or reduced when you are under chronic or constant stress. Recent studies have indicated that people who have a history of cancer in their family (an example being breast cancer) may be more susceptible to the development of malignancy if they remain in a chronically stressful condition.

Positive Stress

Getting that income tax return in on time, cramming for a test, and performing physically beyond normal capabilities are all aspects of positive stress responses. Some people claim that they work better under stress; this may be a real consequence with positive results, but only if people do not place themselves in constant (daily) stressful situations. We have all known people who respond with bursts of energy, increased concentration, and creative ideas when they are put under stress, but afterward such emotional reactions to stress drain off. In between, these people tend to rest and relax, and so they are ready for the next stressful event.

Wouldn't it be wonderful if we could all react in that manner?

Negative Stress

I am talking about negative stress with a capital *N*. Stresses that hit at you on a daily basis are unrelenting and have an intensity that leaves you in a state of upheaval both physically and emotionally. Your body is like the engine on a car. Most cars are capable of driving at maximum speed for short periods of time if you press the accelerator to the floor, but after you've passed the car in front of you or averted some precarious situation, you let up on the accelerator and the engine returns to normal. A negative stress situation is as if you pressed the accelerator of your car all the way to the floor and kept it there. Even the newest, most well-tuned car will soon begin to break down if subjected to the unrelenting stress of maximum performance. Some engines cease completely or blow up (as in a heart attack or a stroke), while some others experience a breakdown of a particular part or system (as in a decreased function of the human body's immune system or its development of ulcers). In many cases, especially if the car is not new, the stress focuses on a weak link like a previously damaged drive shaft or carburetor, and that part of the engine becomes the first to break down. The same holds true with the human body. We can all cope with brief periods of acceleration, but under the constant pressure of unrelenting stress (like constant acceleration), we tend to suffer a massive breakdown or the malfunction of a previously weakened link. The body's weak links may be caused by inheritance, genetic predisposition, previous injury, or ailment.

If you suffered a back injury like the one I did playing college football, whenever you allowed yourself to be overstressed, the stress goes directly to the low back and may appear as increased discomfort. Fortunately, I have learned to recognize and resolve stressful complications in my life. This has helped me to eliminate one of the factors that could adversely affect and increase my back pain. I am not perfect, of course, and there are times when I tend to forget or become complacent in the knowledge that I know how to control stress and its relation to my back pain. I spend time on a fairly regular basis reviewing my reactions to stress to insure that stress does not affect my damaged back.

A Two-Edged Sword.

The sword of stress cuts both ways and, unlike the finest broadswords, becomes sharper with usage. Chronic stress may attack you physically or emotionally and many times in both ways.

A Fact of Life.

Stress is a fact of life. You couldn't avoid all stress even if you were to go live in a cave as a hermit. There would always be the stress of something like bears coming in to live with you or dropping rocks. No one is capable of insulating himself or herself from stress. Even knowing its potential for doing damage to the body and mind, some people do not want to make the effort to learn effective stress-reducing techniques. There are few guarantees in life, but one of them is that if you are a pain sufferer, prolonged chronic stress will cause an increase in your pain.

Managing Stress.

Learning to deal with stresses in your environment and the stresses you create within yourself is a matter of identification, practice, and lifestyle change.

You will never learn to deal effectively with your stress if you are not willing to examine which types of stresses are affecting you. You will need to look at your job, home, and relationships and examine how you feel about yourself in all of these situations. Try to identify the situations in your life that make you feel tense, jumpy, or nervous. Try listening to your body and letting it become a barometer for stressful reactions.

Spend some time examining the stressful events in your life, and use this stress reduction miniprogram as a way of identifying and dealing appropriately with stress responses.

The Pain Relief Formulas and Stress.

Upon your completion of the seven-day program, you will have at your disposal one of the most effective methods known for dealing with chronic stress. You will still be able to gear up for the IRS or that report your boss wanted finished by Thursday morning, but without the adverse chronic stress reactions that would cause an increase in your pain.

The method is simple: Whenever you have identified a stressful event and cannot change the cause of the stress, use your personalized pain relief formula to short-circuit the body's (physical and emotional) negative reaction to the stressful event. If you use the personalized pain relief formula as a method for short-circuiting a stress response, after enough practice it will become an automatic habit and allow you to deal effectively with any stressful situation. Additionally, by learning to deal with stress, you will be eliminating one of the major causes of pain increase.

Reinforce, Reinforce.

Whenever you positively reinforce an event, the chances of that event occurring again are increased. We spend much of our lives looking for all reinforcement from outside of ourselves. From the time we are small children, this reinforcement is provided by parents, teachers, and friends. Much of how we view ourselves becomes dependent upon positive or negative reinforcement. If someone is reinforced negatively over and over, then the person will eventually view himself or herself as negative. Tell yourself enough times that you are worthless, and soon you will truly believe that worthlessness is your main characteristic. In fact, you may believe this so strongly that as a result of your actions other people begin to take this same view.

When you reinforce the positive nature of the Scottsdale Pain Relief Program, your body and mind gradually begin to believe that you can actually perform and take control of your pain relief. No one can reinforce positive thoughts continually without an occasional negative response sneaking into the mind. Make an effort to reinforce on a constant and consistent basis the belief in your ability to obtain pain relief. Do it well and do it often. Your body and mind will then work together to fulfill the prophesy you have created.

Overcoming Your Pain—Depression Cycle.

Since we have already established that pain and depression go hand in hand, you need to do something about taking charge of your depression and removing as much of it as possible from your lifestyle. Read over these suggestions, determine which ones apply directly to you, and begin to take control of your depression.

Develop a sense of order in your life.

Try to be on time for appointments, answer your mail, balance your checkbook, have food in the kitchen, eat regular meals, and obtain enough sleep. Developing order in your life will simplify your existence and allow you enough leftover energy for activities such as the Scottsdale Pain Relief Program, hobbies, and achieving your overall goals. When you organize and accomplish, you reinforce your sense of worth and confidence.

Don't dress depressed.

You should pay careful attention to both your dress and your personal grooming. Depressed people tend to dress emotionally. They may look unkempt or unshaven and tend to put off paying any attention to their personal appearance. Try dressing in brighter colors and spending time on your appearance.

Don't be a giver-upper.

Even when you're down and blue, don't give up on activities. Don't quit school, change your job, or stop an uncompleted project. Major decisions should not be made while you are depressed. If a project appears to be overwhelming, then break it into smaller segments, completing each segment as you go forward.

Use an emotional release.

The best emotional relief will result from a combination of the personalized pain relief formula and the exercise/activity portion of the Scottsdale Pain Relief Program. This will allow you to dissipate some of your internal feelings of frustration or anger.

Treat each day as a new challenge.

Don't spend your time bogged down in past failures. Treat each new day as a challenge, plan for that challenge, and accept any successes you may achieve. If you are not able to accomplish all you hope to, then analyze why you have not met your expectations and then set a new course of action.

Don't talk about your problems.

Try to spend at least one day not talking about your problems either to yourself or anyone else. If you can be successful for one day, then try two and then three. The more you focus on and talk about your problems, the greater will be the chance that you are actually reinforcing your depression.

Eliminate Depressing People.

It would be virtually impossible to eliminate all people who have problems or are depressed from your life, but you can go a long ways toward identifying those people whom you associate with on a daily basis who are generally up individuals and experience less depression. If you spend all of your time around people who are down, then it will be quite easy for you to slip into the quicksand of depression and make it a group experience.

Dumping Your Negative Emotions.

If you are going to learn how to control your pain, then you will have to *dump* your negative emotions. These emotions are usually shown through pessimism, feeling down, never being able to find anything good in anything or anybody, and a general Scrooge-like outlook on life.

If you are a negative thinker, then you are going to have to force yourself to begin looking on the bright side of things. You cannot hope to convince your brain to produce its own built-in painkillers if you spend the majority of your time brainwashing yourself into looking at the negative, unsuccessful side of your existence.

Your Prescription for Living.

Your prescription for living will be to utilize the Lifetime Maintenance Program as a method for living life to its fullest. Here's your prescription:

Practice your personalized pain relief formula as often as possible and under varying situations and circumstances.

Keep up with practice, for the more you practice your personalized pain relief formula, the greater its effectiveness will be.

Through constant practice, allow the personalized pain relief formula to become an automatic habit.

Maintain an appropriate exercise/activity program.

Through the advice of your physician, maintain the most nutritional diet possible.

Accept the challenge to be evaluating constantly your emotional reaction to others and the environment.

Be aware that you are an ever-changing organism in an ever-changing environment and therefore be willing to facilitate and accept change.

The most important part of this prescription: Believe in yourself and your ability to control your pain.

My Final Comments for You.

Most people report that upon completion of the Scottsdale Pain Relief Program there is a slow, but steady, continuation of their success in reducing pain and the associated detrimental psychological consequences.

Although I can't be with you to provide congratulations upon successfully completing the Scottsdale Pain Relief Program, I still would like to give you a sincere "well done.'' But in the same breath, I have to caution you against becoming complacent and forgetting that the Life-time Maintenance Program needs to be performed every day and under varying situations and conditions.

The book has come to an end, but you are only beginning to use the power within you to control pain and gain positive emotions. Your future is now up to you.

About the Author

Dr. Neal H. Olshan is a psychologist who works with pain victims. He is the author of *Fears and Phobias: Fighting Back*, *Depression*, *Phobia Free and Flying High*, and *Power Over Your Pain Without Drugs*. He lives with his family in Scottsdale, Arizona.